SOUTHERN
AND
EASTERN
ASIA

The Great Wall of China at Shanxi, China

SOUTHERN AND EASTERN ASIA

Martyn Bramwell

Lerner Publications Company • Minneapolis

**First American edition published in 2000
by Lerner Publications Company**

© 2000 by Graham Beehag Books

Lerner Publications Company
A division of Lerner Publishing Group
241 First Avenue North
Minneapolis, MN 55401 U.S.A.

Website address: www.lernerbooks.com

Library of Congress Cataloging-in-Publication Data

Bramwell, Martyn.
  Southern and eastern Asia / by Martyn Bramwell.
    p. cm. — (The world in maps)
Includes index.
  ISBN 0-8225-2916-5 (lib. bdg. : alk. paper)
1. South Asia—Geography--Juvenile literature. 2. East
Asia—Geography—Juvenile literature. 3. Asia, Southeastern—
Geography—Juvenile literature. [1. South Asia. 2. East
Asia. 3. Asia, Southeastern.] I. Title. II. Series: Bramwell, Martyn.
The world in maps.
  DS336.9 .B73 2000
  915—dc21   00-010576

Printed in Singapore by Tat Wei Printing Packaging Pte Ltd
Bound in the United States of America
1 2 3 4 5 6 – OS – 05 04 03 02 01 00

CONTENTS

Southern and Eastern Asia   6

China   8

Hong Kong and Macao   14

Taiwan   15

Mongolia   16

North Korea and South Korea   18

Japan   20

Philippines   24

Indonesia   26

Malaysia, Singapore, Brunei   28

Vietnam, Laos, Cambodia   30

Myanmar and Thailand   32

India   34

Bangladesh, Sri Lanka, Maldives   40

Nepal and Bhutan   42

Pakistan and Afghanistan   44

Glossary   46

Index   48

SOUTHERN and EASTERN ASIA

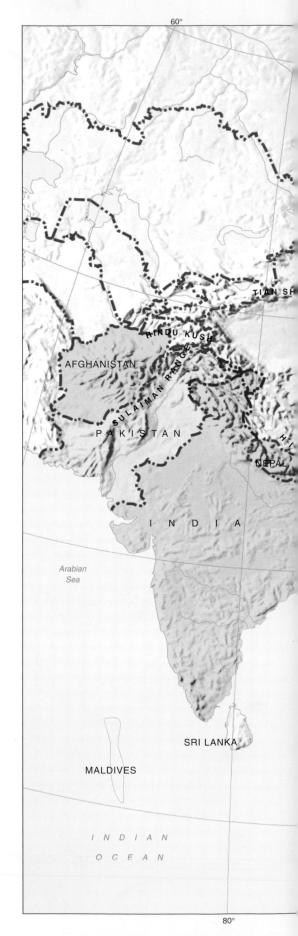

The southern and eastern sections of the huge Asian continent comprise a land area that contains almost every kind of landscape imaginable, and every climatic extreme on earth. A kaleidoscope of peoples with widely different languages, religions, lifestyles, and economic conditions make their homes in these parts of Asia.

Southern and eastern Asia stretches west to east for more than 3,700 miles, from Pakistan to the Pacific coast of China. North to south covers 4,000 miles from China's northern border with Russia to the tropical islands of Indonesia. Mount Everest, the world's highest mountain, towers 29,028 feet above sea level in the eastern Himalayas, while some of the world's deepest ocean trenches plunge six and a half miles below sea level off Japan and the Philippines.

Vast rolling **steppes,** high **plateaus,** and huge deserts dominate the western and northern parts of the region. To the south and east, densely forested mountains and hills cover much of the land. Some of the world's mightiest rivers—the Ganges, the Brahmaputra, the Mekong, the Chang (Yangtze), and the Huang He (Yellow)—pass powerfully through the region, crossing fertile coastal plains and broad **deltas** to reach the ocean.

The peoples and lifestyles of southern and eastern Asia are as varied as their landscapes. Mongolia's livestock farmers graze their sheep and cattle on vast plains. Rice farmers in the mountains of the Philippines plant their crops on small steep hillside **terraces** constructed 2,000 years ago. Factory workers in many southern Asian countries work from dawn till dusk for very low wages. And hunger, water shortages, and inadequate health and educational services are facts of life for millions. But alongside the nations with fewer services are some of the world's most powerful and dynamic economies. Japan is one of the world's leading manufacturers of cars, electronic goods, textiles, and household appliances. Farther south are other world-ranking industrial and commercial centers, including Taiwan, Singapore, and Hong Kong (part of China).

In addition to economic powerhouses, there are population powerhouses in southern and eastern Asia, too. India and China together are home to 37 percent of the world's population. With the populations of Indonesia and Bangladesh added in, these four nations alone account for 43 percent of the world's people—but they all inhabit a combined land area that represents just 8 percent of the earth's total. These sorts of contrasts make southern and eastern Asia among the most complex areas of the world.

China

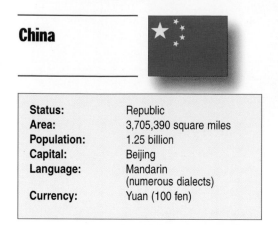
China has by far the largest population of any nation in the world, with more than 1.25 billion people. It is also one of the world's largest countries by land area. China's vast territory is also enormously varied in topography and climate. The rugged Tian Shan (mountains), the Pamir Mountains, and the Karakoram Mountains rise in the west, forming a high, cold, rocky barrier between China and Kazakhstan, Kyrgyzstan, Tajikistan, and Pakistan. The eastern part of the Tian Shan range extends across northwestern China, becoming the Mongolian Uplands—a dry, high desert region with few inhabitants. The Gobi Desert's stony expanse forms part of this arid plateau. Daytime temperatures in the deserts can soar past 100°F in summer, plunging to -30°F during the icy winter nights.

North and east of the highlands lie large areas of **loess**—fine, yellowish soil formed from the clay deposits left behind by **glaciers,** then blown around by the wind and dumped in thick layers. The soils, though fertile, are soft and easily eroded. One of China's great rivers, the Huang He (Yellow River) flows across this region. The river takes its name from the huge amounts of yellow mud that stain its waters. Little rain falls in northern China, and the winters are long and very cold. Average January temperatures drop well below freezing. Farmers in the north concentrate on hardy crops like winter wheat, corn, and millet.

The towering Himalayas and the lofty Plateau of Tibet dominate southwestern China. The Himalayas contain the world's highest peak, Mount Everest, which at 29,028 feet is a legendary mountain to climb. Most of the plateau consists of bare rock, gravel, and snowfields, but farmers are able to graze hardy yaks on the sparse mountain pastures. They also grow vegetables and grains in some of the sheltered valleys and low-lying areas.

China's Eastern Lowlands form a long narrow north-south belt of hilly country that is dissected by broad river valleys such as the Chang (Yangtze).

Below: With the hills of the Mongolian Uplands in the distance, a goatherd tends his flock.

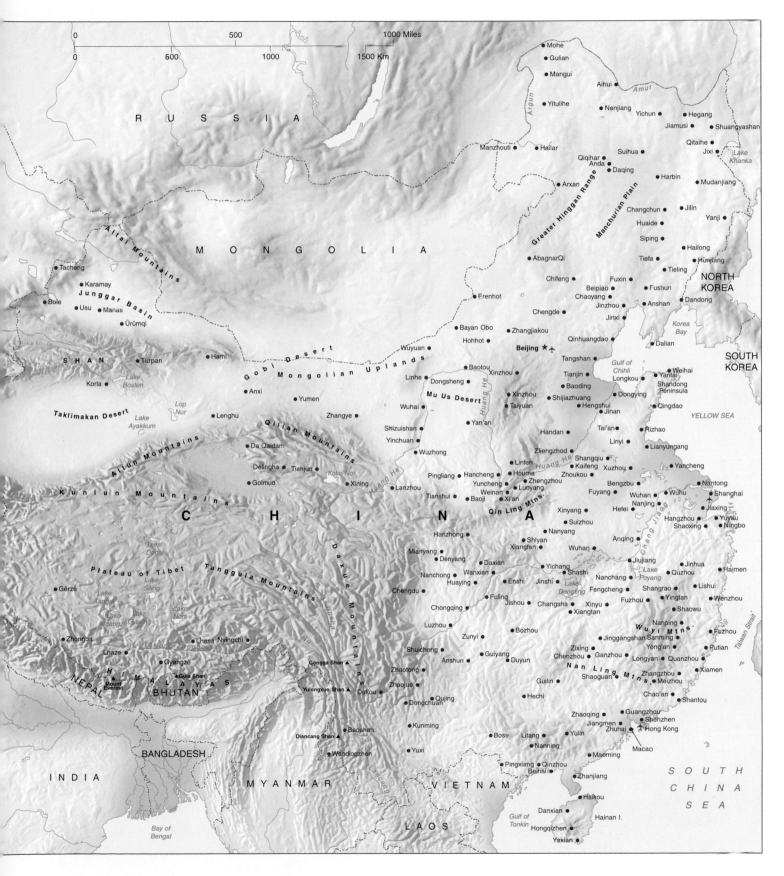

China

The lowlands support much of China's most productive cropland. Farmers grow wheat, rice, and vegetables, and raise cattle, pigs, and poultry. These lowlands also contain some of China's largest coalfields and iron ore deposits. Extensive forests wedged between the lowlands and the Pacific coast supply premium timber for construction projects. Just beyond the trees, the coast is dotted with several natural deepwater harbors.

A small, circular lowland called the Sichuan Basin, on the eastern edge of the Plateau of Tibet, provides a second important agricultural region. The climate here is mild, and the hilly land is broken up with fertile valleys. Most farmers cultivate terraced fields to make the best use of every available acre. Primary crops are rice, corn, potatoes, cabbage, apples, pears, sugar beets, soybeans, and tea. Nonfood crops include rubber, cotton, and tobacco.

Below: Flooded rice fields, known as rice paddies, cover much of the Xi Jiang Valley in the Guangxi region of southeastern China.

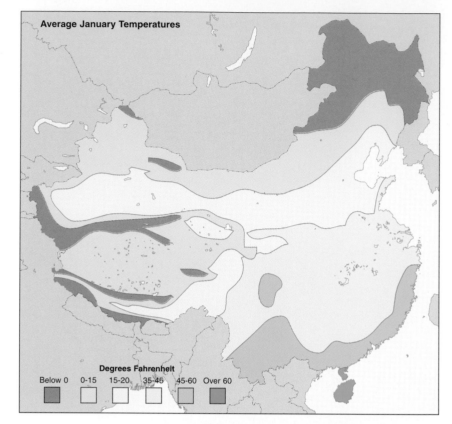

Average January Temperatures

Degrees Fahrenheit

Below 0   0-15   15-20   35-45   45-60   Over 60

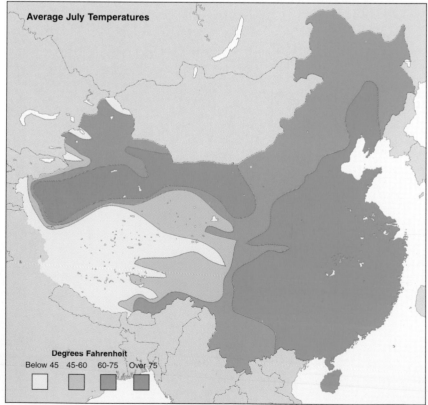

Average July Temperatures

Degrees Fahrenheit

Below 45   45-60   60-75   Over 75

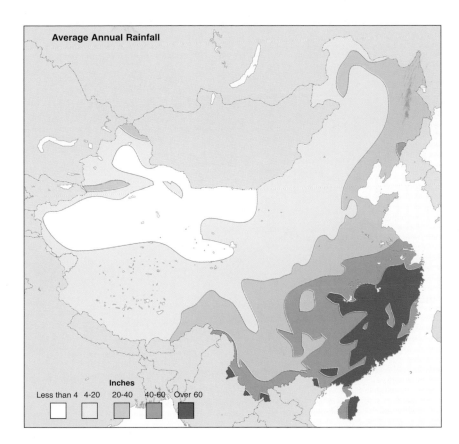

Average Annual Rainfall

Inches

Less than 4 | 4-20 | 20-40 | 40-60 | Over 60

Steep wooded hills and rocky mountains cover most of southeastern China. Much of the land is too steep for farming, but the valleys contain good cropland. The wide delta of the Xi Jiang (West River)—southern China's principal waterway—supports deep, fertile soil. Southeastern China enjoys a tropical climate with mild winters, hot summers, and plentiful rainfall. Farmers there grow many varieties of grains, vegetables, and fruits and tend large herds of cattle, sheep, goats, pigs, chickens, and ducks. China's farmers raise about one-third of the world's pigs, using them not only for their meat but also for their manure, which is an excellent fertilizer.

Roughly one-fifth of the world's population lives in China, but the people are distributed unevenly. Only about 10 percent of the population live in western China, settling in the valleys and foothills that ring the mountainous western and southern borders.

Below: The Palace of Heavenly Purity, built in 1420, is one of the finest buildings in Beijing's Forbidden City.

China

The deserts and plateaus of west central China appear even emptier, with less than five people per square mile. People along these borderlands—**subsistence farmers** and livestock herders—include a mix of ethnic Chinese and several minority ethnic groups, such as Kazakhs, Mongols, Uygurs, and Tibetans.

Eastern China is much more densely populated, with an average of up to 1,000 people per square mile. About 80 percent of the eastern inhabitants live in small farming villages scattered across the land. Many of these communities belong to a cooperative system, in which a large group of members decides which crops and livestock each family farm will produce. After the harvest, part of the crop is sold to the government, and part of it goes to the community for sale or distribution. Any surplus can be eaten by the family or sold in the local market. Farming is not highly mechanized, and the people work long hours, often using simple hand tools. Horses, oxen, handcarts, and bicycles are common transportation options. Most rural families live in single-story houses of mud or clay brick, with a thatched or tile roof. There are few luxuries, but most homes have electricity, and most villages have schools, libraries, and community centers.

China also has some of the world's largest and most crowded cities. Shanghai has nearly 12 million people, the capital of Beijing supports 10 million, and more than 30 other cities house at least 1 million people each. Most major Chinese cities have built large, new apartment complexes alongside the older houses. Living units are small, but most people have enough income to meet their needs, and all have access to education, health care, and community services.

City dwellers work in manufacturing, in shops, in service industries, in transportation, in education, and in government administration. Shanghai is the principal manufacturing center, followed by Beijing, Tianjin, and Shenyang in the north; Guangahou, Hangzhou, and Wuhan in the south; and Chongqing and Chengdu in east central China. Factory workers produce industrial and farm machinery, vehicles, textiles, fertilizer, cement, chemicals, and household goods such as sewing machines, televisions, and furniture. China has developed many hydroelectric plants that provide 20 percent of its power needs. The remainder comes from vast coalfields in the north and northeast and large oil fields in Manchuria, near Tianjin, and on the Shandong Peninsula. Miners also extract huge quantities of iron ore, tungsten, antimony, lead, and tin.

Throughout most of its long history, China remained isolated from the rest of the world.

The mountain ranges, forests, and deserts that encircle most of its western and southern borders cut off China from western Asia and Europe. The Pacific Ocean formed a natural barrier between China and the developing world of North America. This geographical separation, combined with an ancient Chinese policy of discouraging contact with other countries, meant that the country's culture, traditions, and internal politics remained unaffected by world events well into the nineteenth century.

Powerful dynasties (ruling families) governed the Chinese Empire from the third century B.C. until the eighteenth century, when a dramatic rise in the population and a succession of failed harvests led to widespread suffering and political unrest. The great empire began to crumble and fall apart. Wars with Britain and Japan in the nineteenth century hastened the empire's collapse, and in 1912 China's last emperor abdicated. China became a chaotic republic ruled by army generals, powerful regional governors, and local warlords. After almost 40 years of civil hostilities and a long war with Japan, the **Communist** leader Mao Zedong took control in 1949, founding the People's Republic of China.

Since Mao's death in 1976, his successors have continued to insist on total government control, but they have also recognized the need for economic growth. They have encouraged foreign investment and have increased trade with Japan, the United States, and Germany. The government has set up special economic zones where foreign firms can establish businesses in China. The government also continues the staggering task of modernizing China's agriculture, industry, infrastructure, and urban areas.

Above: Chinese farmers thresh their rice crop with traditional hand tools.

Below: Rural communities depend almost entirely on wood for fuel.

13

Hong Kong and Macao

Hong Kong lies at the mouth of the Zhu Jiang (Pearl River) about 90 miles southeast of Guangzhou. It is comprised of a mountainous peninsula jutting from mainland China and 235 islands—the largest of which is Hong Kong Island, the territory's capital and commercial center.

Leased to Britain in 1898, Hong Kong was returned to Chinese rule with great ceremony in 1997. It forms an important part of modern China's expanding economy. Most of its people work in banking and financial services, tourism, international trade, and manufacturing—sending watches, textiles and clothing, electronic equipment, and plastic goods all over the world.

The tiny territory of Macao, including the nearby islands of Colóane and Taipa, lies about 40 miles west of Hong Kong. Portuguese traders settled in Macao in 1557, and for the next 200 years the city and its port dominated the international trade in silk, spices, and other goods. A treaty with China recognized the settlement as Portuguese territory in 1887. Portugal returned Macao to Chinese rule in 1997. More than 90 percent of Macao's people are Chinese. Most of the rest are Portuguese.

Macao's thriving capitalist economy benefits China, which supplies virtually all Macao's food, fresh water, and energy needs and buys manufactured goods from the region. Tourism and light industry are Macao's main economic activities. Factory workers produce textiles and fireworks, which are exported to China and countries all over the world. Hotel staff, restaurant workers, and taxi drivers support a successful tourist industry. Around six million tourists visit Macao each year—almost 80 percent of them from Hong Kong.

Below: Fishermen navigate their boats among the floating homes in the harbor of Macao.

Bottom: The view across Hong Kong's busy harbor, from Hong Kong Island to Kowloon on the mainland

Taiwan

Taiwan

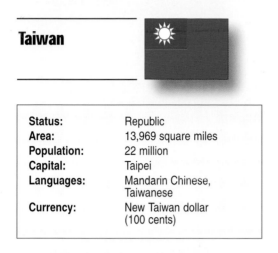

Status:	Republic
Area:	13,969 square miles
Population:	22 million
Capital:	Taipei
Languages:	Mandarin Chinese, Taiwanese
Currency:	New Taiwan dollar (100 cents)

The 250-mile-long island of Taiwan lies astride the **Tropic of Cancer,** about 90 miles off the Chinese coast. It has a warm, moist climate through most of the year, with heavy monsoon rains between June and August. The highest mountains receive snow in the winter. Mountains extend along the whole length of Taiwan, dominating the central and eastern parts and rising to 12,000 feet in places. Evergreen forests of camphor, hemlock, and cork oak cover the lower slopes of the mountains, with cedar, larch, and pine forests taking over higher up.

Along the eastern coast, the mountains slope down steeply to the sea, creating a rugged coastline with a very narrow coastal plain. By contrast, along the western coast, low rolling hills reach down to a broad, fertile plain and provide Taiwan's only large area of lowland. Most of the population live in the towns and cities of the west, where most of the island's agriculture also takes place. A bit farther inland are fertile valleys, where farmers build terraces into the hillsides to create more land for cultivation. Taiwan's principal crops are rice, maize, bananas, citrus fruits, asparagus, sweet potatoes, and other vegetables, sugarcane, and tea. Chickens, ducks, and pigs are the most common livestock. Coastal fishing crews bring in shrimp, tuna, and other fish for the local markets.

Taiwan is not rich in mineral resources, but the island's miners produce modest quantities of coal, copper, gold, silver, sulfur, and salt. Limestone quarries produce hard stone for building houses and roads, and oil and gas wells contribute to the country's energy needs. Most raw materials, however, are imported. Manufacturing industries in the larger towns produce electronic goods such as calculators, television sets, and radios. They also make textiles and clothing, plastics, toys, and a wide range of forest products—bamboo, lumber, plywood, paper, and wooden furniture.

Above: Electronics manufacturing is an important part of the Taiwanese economy.

Mongolia

Mongolia

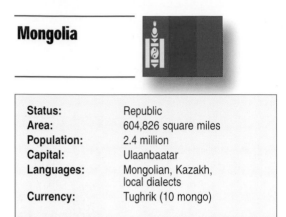

Status:	Republic
Area:	604,826 square miles
Population:	2.4 million
Capital:	Ulaanbaatar
Languages:	Mongolian, Kazakh, local dialects
Currency:	Tughrik (10 mongo)

Mongolia, sandwiched between Russia and China in eastern central Asia, is the world's largest landlocked country. Spanning 1,500 miles from east to west and nearly 800 miles from north to south, it is larger than Alaska. Yet Mongolia is one of the world's most sparsely populated countries, with an average of less than four people per square mile. It is a harsh, rugged country of mountain ranges, upland plateaus, windswept plains, and deserts. Mongolia's climate is typical of a highland region far from the softening influence of the sea. Summers are short and often hot, with temperatures up to 100°F. Winters are long, windy, and bitterly cold, with temperatures dropping to -55°F. Heavy snowfalls are common in the mountainous regions.

Mountains and high steppes dominate northern Mongolia. The Altai Shan rise above 14,000 feet on Mongolia's border with China, and the Hangayn Mountains stretch across the country's middle. The densely forested Hentiyn Nuruu extends northeastward from the capital city of Ulaanbaatar to the Russian border. A high undulating plateau dotted with lakes and forests covers northwestern Mongolia. The country's largest body of water, Uvs Nuur, has an area of more than 1,300 square miles. Lower plains of semi-arid grassland cover the east, gradually becoming more arid as they merge with the barren expanse of the Gobi Desert, which stretches across much of Mongolia's border with China.

The country's people boast a long history of herding livestock. Traditionally nomadic, they constantly shifted their cattle, horses, sheep, goats, and camels from one grazing area to another. Their homes were circular tentlike structures called yurts that were made of thick felt mats fixed over a frame of bent poles. Yurts could be dismantled for transportation, but some early pictures show them being carried on large carts pulled by oxen.

The ancient people of Mongolia, the Mongols, possessed unmatched skill with horses and bows and arrows. Their warlike character made them a major force in the Mongol Empire of Genghis Khan, which dominated Asia through the Middle Ages (A.D. 500 to A.D. 1500). Herding livestock has replaced both the warring skills and the nomadic lifestyle as the principal farming activity in Mongolia and a mainstay of the economy. Most of the population have settled in small villages that dot the vast grazing lands. Mongolians raise more than 20 million head of livestock—about half of them sheep. Cattle, wool, hides, and dairy products comprise the country's principal exports. Mutton, beef, milk,

Below: Mongolian men make felt from sheep's wool while sitting outside a traditional yurt.

and cheese form the basis of the national diet. In the country's hilly north, farmers plant grains and vegetables in the fertile black soil.

From 1921 to 1990, Mongolia was a Communist state dependent on the Soviet Union for financial assistance. Mining and manufacturing grew rapidly during this period, eventually contributing as much to the country's economy as agriculture did. When the Soviet Union broke apart in 1991, Mongolia's financial aid dried up. The country continued to develop its mining interests, producing coal, oil, iron ore, copper, molybdenum, tin, gold, lead, and other minerals. Factory workers made textiles, glass, ceramics, timber products, and other goods. But economic growth has faltered, and the country has been unable to continue modernizing its industries and transportation systems without additional funding.

Above: The magnificent walled temple of Karakorum Erdeni Dzu is set against the vast landscape of the Mongolian Plain.

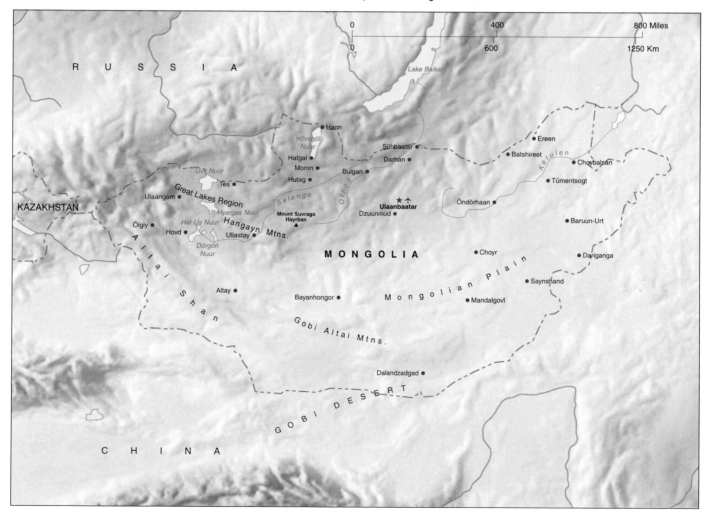

North Korea and South Korea

Two nations—North Korea and South Korea—occupy the mountainous 670-mile-long Korean Peninsula, which juts southward from the coast of eastern Asia. The Sea of Japan lies to the east of the peninsula. To the west extend Korea Bay and the Yellow Sea. The Korea Strait, south of the peninsula, separates South Korea from the northern tip of Japan. About 3,000 islands, most of them dotting the waters west and south of the peninsula, belong to the two countries. North Korea shares its northern border almost entirely with China. Just one short section in the extreme northeast is shared with Russia.

Before World War II (1939–1945), Korea was one nation but had been occupied by Japan since 1910. By the war's end, Japan had relinquished control, and Korea had separated into two nations. North Korea adopted a Communist regime, while South Korea was strongly anti-Communist. Friction between the two followed, and in 1950 North Korea invaded South Korea, igniting the Korean War. China and the Soviet Union supported North Korea. The United States and other non-Communist countries assisted South Korea. The war ended in 1953, but a permanent peace treaty has not been signed. In the spring of 2000, the first direct meeting between the leaders of the two Koreas signaled a possible end to the stalemate.

Above: The "Bridge of No Return" border crossing, near Panmunjom in North Korea

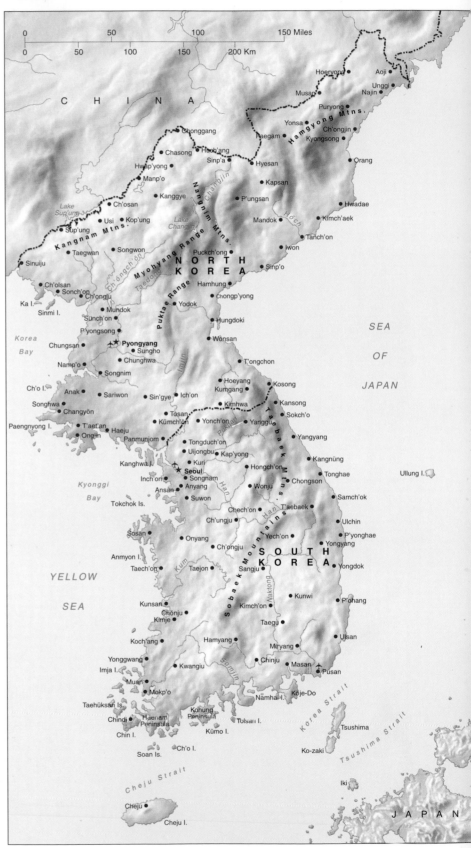

Democratic People's Republic of Korea
(North Korea)

Status:	Republic
Area:	46,541 square miles
Population:	21.4 million
Capital:	Pyongyang
Language:	Korean
Currency:	North Korean won (100 zeuns)

Republic of Korea
(South Korea)

Status:	Republic
Area:	38,324 square miles
Population:	46.9 million
Capital:	Seoul
Language:	Korean
Currency:	South Korean won (100 chon)

Three distinct land regions divide North Korea. A broad plain subdivided by low hills parallels the western coast, providing most of North Korea's best farmland. Government-organized co-operatives divide the land into farming communities of up to 300 families. Each family works a section of the land, earning a portion of the harvest and a small income. The bulk of the produce is given to the government for distribution to the cities. Principal cooperative crops include rice, corn, millet, potatoes, and other vegetables. Most farmers also raise chickens and pigs. Roughly half the North Koreans reside in this western region—about two million of them in the capital city of Pyongyang.

Forested mountains cover central North Korea. The country's largest region has a small population and virtually no agriculture. Residents support their families by mining many of the country's raw materials and by cutting timber for construction, furniture, and plywood and paper production.

In the east, a narrow band of coastal lowlands faces the Sea of Japan. About one-quarter of the country's people live in the area, farming North Korea's second most productive farmland area.

Monsoon rains and winter snows provide 30 to 60 inches of precipitation each year, enough to meet the needs of both rural and urban populations. The country's industrial strength is based on mining, iron and steel, machinery, chemicals, and textiles. Miners dig copper, iron ore, lead, zinc, and tungsten, much of it for export to China, Japan, and Russia.

Right: Pusan is one of the principal cities on the southeastern coast of South Korea.

South Korea has two principal land regions. Wide, flat plains separated by ribbons of rolling hills form a broad band around the western and southern coasts. Central and eastern South Korea is covered in densely forested mountains. The fertile, well-irrigated coastal plains support most of South Korea's agriculture. In sharp contrast to state-run North Korea, southern farms are almost entirely small, privately owned family businesses. The farmers supplement the primary crop of rice with barley and a great variety of vegetables, including white radishes, onions, cabbages, sweet potatoes, and fruits such as apples and oranges. Farmers in the mountain regions cultivate every spare foot of land possible. They terrace the hillsides, farm the valley floors, and plant crops in the few small areas of lowland along the eastern coast. South Korea's large fishing fleet catches a variety of fish and seafood for local and international markets.

About three-quarters of South Koreans inhabit the coastal plains, where manufacturing and service industries provide about 75 percent of the country's jobs. In the 1950s, North Korea dominated the peninsula's industrial force. South Korea invested heavily in both traditional and high-tech industries, overtaking North Korea as a major producer and worldwide exporter of iron and steel, ships, cars, machinery, chemicals, and tires. The country also manufactures and exports computers, audio and video equipment, cameras, household electrical goods, textiles, and clothing.

Japan

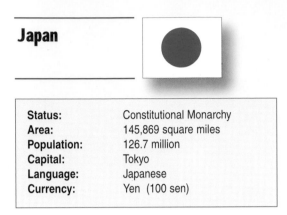

Japan

Status:	Constitutional Monarchy
Area:	145,869 square miles
Population:	126.7 million
Capital:	Tokyo
Language:	Japanese
Currency:	Yen (100 sen)

Four large islands—Hokkaido, Honshu, Shikoku, and Kyushu—account for nearly 98 percent of Japan's land area. These islands lie in a 1,180-mile-long arc off the Asian mainland, facing Russia, North and South Korea, and China across the Sea of Japan and the East China Sea. Japan's remaining 2 percent of land includes about 4,000 smaller islands. Some nestle near the coasts of the main islands. Others, such as the Izu Islands, reach far into the Pacific Ocean. And the Ryukyu Islands extend like a string of pearls from Kyushu Island southwestward almost to Taiwan.

Japan's islands lie above one of the most geologically active sections of the earth's crust. Far beneath the island chains, a section of seabed is dragging another down and beneath it. As the seabed grinds, earthquakes—1,500 each year—jolt Japan's landscape and people. Most quakes are minor tremors, causing little or no damage, but every few years a large earthquake strikes, causing extensive damage and casualties. The earthquake of January 17, 1995, rocked the industrial city of Kobe at the southern tip of Honshu Island. The quake destroyed at least 103,000 homes, killed more than 5,000 people, injured 27,000, and left one-fifth of the city's population homeless.

Below: Bridges, water, cherry blossoms, and colorful foliage are among the components of traditional Japanese formal gardens.

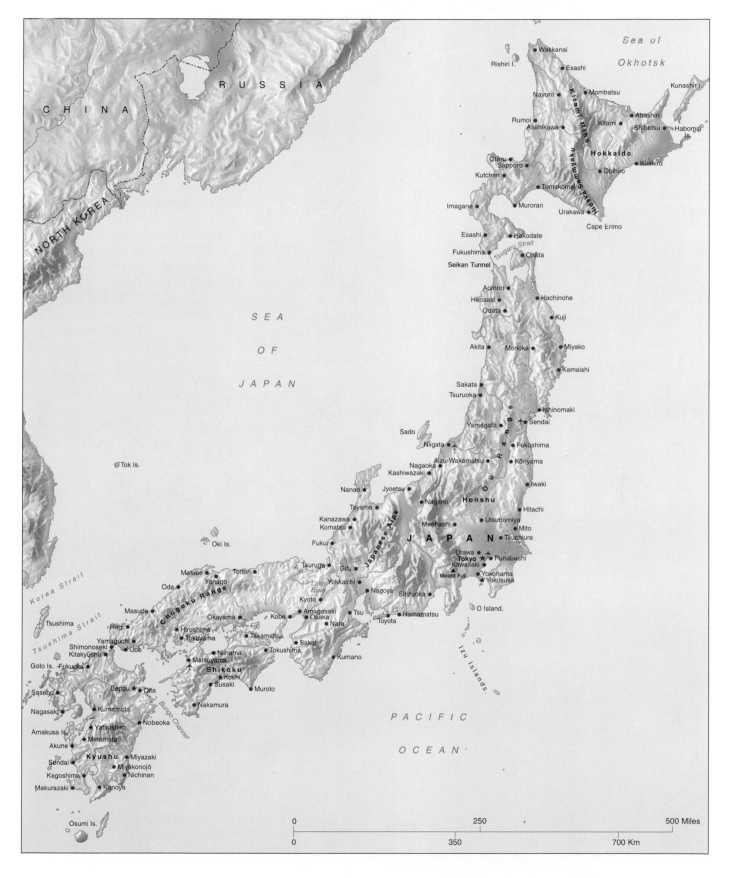

Sea of
Okhotsk

RUSSIA

CHINA

Wakkanai
Rishiri I.
Esashi

Nayoro
Mombatsu
Kunashir I.

Rumoi
Asahikawa
Kitami
Abashiri
Shibetsu
Habomai
Is.

NORTH KOREA

Otaru
Sapporo
Hokkaido
Kushiro
Kutchan
Obihiro

Imagane
Tomakomai
Muroran
Urakawa
Cape Erimo

Esashi
Hakodate
Tsugaru Strait
Fukushima
Ohata
Seikan Tunnel

Aomori
Hirosaki
Hachinohe
Odata
Kuji

Akita
Morioka
Miyako

SEA
Kamaishi

OF
Sakata
Tsuruoka
Ishinomaki

JAPAN
Yamagata
Sendai

Sado
Fukushima
Niigata
Kōriyama

Aizu-Wakamatsu
Nagaoka
Tok Is.
Kashiwazaki
Iwaki

Nanao
Jyoetsu
Honshu

Toyama
Nagano
Hitachi

Kanazawa
Maebashi
Utsunomiya
Mito

Komatsu
JAPAN
Tsuchiura

Fukui
Urawa
Tokyo
Funabashi
Kawasaki

Oki Is.
Tsuruga
Gifu
Mount Fuji
Yokohama
Yokosuka

Matsue
Yonago
Tottori
Yokkaichi

Oda
Lake Biwa
Nagoya
O Island.

Masuda
Chugoku Range
Kyoto
Shizuoka

Okayama
Kobe
Tsu
Hamamatsu

Hiroshima
Amagasaki
Nara
Toyota

Hagi
Tokuyama
Osaka

Yamaguchi
Takamatsu
Sakai
Kumano

Shimonoseki
Niihama
Tokushima

Kitakyushu
Ube
Matsuyama

Goto Is.
Fukuoka
Shikoku
Kochi

Sasebo
Beppu
Oita
Susaki
Muroto

Nagasaki
Kumamoto
Nakamura

Amakusa Is.
Yatsushiro
Nobeoka

Akune
Minamata

Sendai
Kyushu
Miyazaki

Kagoshima
Miyakonojō
Nichinan

Makurazaki
Kanoya

Osumi Is.

PACIFIC

OCEAN

Izu Islands

Korea Strait

Tsushima

Tsushima Strait

| 0 | | 250 | | 500 Miles |

| 0 | | 350 | | 700 Km |

21

Japan

Left: Downtown Tokyo is noisy, colorful, and busy at all hours of the day and night.

Volcanoes are another geologic component of Japanese life. The islands are actually the tops of a huge range of volcanic mountains rising from the Pacific seabed. More than 150 large volcanoes peek above the ocean's surface, and about half of them are still active (capable of erupting). Mount Fuji, an inactive volcano, forms Japan's highest summit, rising to 12,388 feet above sea level on Honshu Island.

Spectacular mountains, rolling hills, and precious forests cover much of Japan, providing stunning scenery for the country's many visitors. Nearly 70 percent of the land is mountainous, so Japan's 126 million people tend to concentrate near the coasts, where narrow plains provide space for urban development. The most heavily inhabited areas lie along the Pacific coast of Honshu Island, where major cities, industrial centers, and ports have developed around deep sheltered bays. Tokyo's metropolitan area houses more than 12 million people, and the surrounding area holds another 6 million. Osaka's residents number nearly 10 million. Other major urban areas include Yokohama, Nagoya, Osaka, and Kyoto.

Despite its small size, Japan has one of the world's strongest economies. The country's gross domestic product (GDP)—the total value of all the goods and services produced within the country in a year—is second only to that of the United States. Japan has achieved this rank with relatively few natural resources. Japanese miners extract small quantities of coal, lead, tin, zinc, manganese, silver, and other minerals. But Japan imports most of its copper and aluminum and nearly all the coking coal and iron ore used in its huge iron and steel industry. Japan produces steel for its own use as well as manufacturing steel sheets, rolls, pipes, and wire for export. The country's powerful industrial economy is built on three crucial steps—import raw materials; turn them into high-value, high-quality products; and

Center: Tokyo shoppers examine the latest goods on display in a downtown electronics store.

Left: Japan's famous bullet trains are part of a rail transport system that the operators proudly claim is the most reliable and punctual in the world.

export those goods all over the world. This approach has moved Japan to the forefront of the world's trading nations.

About one-quarter of Japan's workforce is employed in manufacturing industries. Automobiles are among the country's principal exports. More than 8 million of them are produced annually. Japan is also the world's leading shipbuilder and a major supplier of heavy machinery, such as cranes, turbines, machine tools, and electrical equipment. Factory workers create cameras, watches, scientific instruments, audio and video equipment, computers, calculators, washing machines, and many other household goods. Textiles, ceramics, paper, and wood products are also exported, and the country's petrochemical industries—using oil and natural gas as raw materials—produce a wide range of plastic, and synthetic fibers for the textile trade. The five principal manufacturing regions are Tokyo–Yokohama; Nagoya–Yokkaichi; Kobe–Kyoto–Osaka; and Niihama–Hiroshima–Fukuyama–Okayama, all on the Pacific coast, and Komatsu–Toyama–Niigata on the coast of the Sea of Japan.

More than half the Japanese are employed in one of the service industries—working as health-care providers, teachers, bank tellers, insurance agents, telephone operators, and hotel and restaurant workers. Many work as tour guides for the country's thriving tourist industry.

Japan's climate varies a great deal from north to south. Residents of Hokkaido experience cool summers and bitterly cold winters, often with thick snowfalls. Honshu has warm, humid summers and winters that get more mild farther south. As the southernmost large island, Kyushu enjoys a warm, temperate climate, with hot summers and mild winters. Most of Japan receives ample rainfall to meet the needs of both city dwellers and farmers. Only Hokkaido's eastern side has a markedly dry climate.

Japan makes productive use of its relatively sparse farmland. Farmers have boosted productivity by irrigating, by terracing hillsides, by choosing high-yield crop strains, and by using large amounts of fertilizer. Rice is the country's most significant crop and the basis of its national diet. Japanese farmers grow many varieties of vegetables and fruits, and many raise poultry, pigs, and cattle. Some farmers specialize in nonfood crops such as tobacco and mulberry

trees, whose leaves are used to feed silkworms. Japan's agriculture sector produces almost 70 percent of the country's food needs. The remainder is imported.

With a long coastline and hundreds of bays and inlets, Japan has a long tradition of fishing and the largest fishing fleet in the world, estimated at more than 400,000 vessels. Traditional fishers with small boats work the coastal waters, while the large modern deepsea trawlers, **seiners,** and squid-catchers roam the oceans. Fish has long been Japan's principal source of animal protein, and nutritionists believe that the combination of rice, fish, and vegetables in the Japanese diet has long protected the population from the high incidence of heart disease seen in other developed countries.

Above: Japan has a rich and complex theatrical tradition dating back many centuries.

Left: Elegant Japanese cuisine combines fresh ingredients and perfect presentation. Rural Japanese are more likely to dine on boiled rice and a few vegetables.

Philippines

Philippines

Status:	Republic
Area:	115,830 square miles
Population:	74.7 million
Capital:	Manila
Languages:	Tagalog, English, Spanish, Cebuano
Currency:	Filipino peso (100 centavos)

Above: Hillside rice terraces in northern Luzon

Opposite inset: Modern buildings dominate the center of Manila.

The Philippines consists of more than 7,100 islands set in the western Pacific Ocean between Taiwan to the north and Indonesia to the south. The island group extends 1,150 miles north to south, nearly 700 miles west to east, and has almost 11,000 miles of coastline. About 1,000 of the islands are inhabited. Most Filipinos live on the two largest islands—Luzon at the northern end and Mindanao in the south—and on the cluster of medium-sized islands called the Visayas that lie between them. About half the total population lives on Luzon, with the greatest concentration in and around the capital city of Manila.

Mountains dominate the interior of most of the larger islands, with lowland plains fringing the coasts. The only large inland plains are on Luzon and Panay, where fertile soils support the islands' most productive rice farms. The Philippine Islands were formed by volcanoes, and more than 20 of them are still active. Mount Pinatubo, northwest of Manila Bay, erupted in 1991 in one of the most violent volcanic eruptions of the past century. Forests cover about half the total land area, providing the islands with a valuable resource. Philippine mahogany is exported worldwide, and pine and bamboo are used for large- and small-scale construction projects. **Kapok,** the cottonlike fiber that covers the seedpods of the ceiba tree, is harvested and exported for use as an insulation material and for stuffing furniture.

Spain founded a **colony** in the Philippines (named for King Philip II of Spain) in 1566 and governed the islands for the next 300 years. The United States took control in 1898 and made the islands a self-governing commonwealth in 1935. The Philippines became fully independent in 1946.

The Philippines' population contains many different ethnic groups. Most Filipinos are descended from early immigrants from Indonesia and Malaya. Others are descended from more recent arrivals from China, India, Japan, Europe, and North America. A few large groups dominate the lowlands and cities of the main islands, but the mountainous regions are home to many smaller groups who speak more than 100 local languages and dialects and have their own distinctive traditions and cultures.

The islands' fertile volcanic soils and hot, damp, tropical climate make the land very productive. Filipino farmers grow most of the food the country needs. Rice and corn are the staple food crops. Others include cassava, sweet potatoes, mangoes, and bananas. Cacao beans, coffee beans, pineapples, sugarcane, **hemp,** and tobacco are grown for use within the Philippines and also for export. Farmers also raise large numbers of cattle, water buffalo, pigs, goats, and hens. Most of the crops are grown on the plains, but the northern part of Luzon also contains some of Asia's most spectacular hillside rice terraces, some of which were built more than 2,000 years ago. As well as producing food, these remarkable fields are a major tourist attraction, along with the islands' stunning scenery, wild flowers and birds, and beautiful beaches.

Fishing is a major industry in this island nation. Fishing crews catch sardines, mackerel, tuna, and many other fish offshore, and crabs, shellfish, and sponges are harvested from the shallow coastal waters. Fish farmers raise shrimp and tilapia, a popular food fish, in artificial ponds constructed along the shores.

Mining and manufacturing are the fastest-growing sectors of the economy. Miners produce copper, nickel, and gold for export, but the islands also contain large reserves of chromite, lead, silver, manganese, and zinc that have yet to be exploited. Food processing is the largest industry. Newer industries include textiles, clothing and shoes, electrical and electronic goods, and furniture.

The economy of the Philippines is still developing, but government projects over the past 20 years have improved housing, health care, water supplies, and sanitation. Almost 90 percent of the population can read and write, and nearly all school-age children attend school.

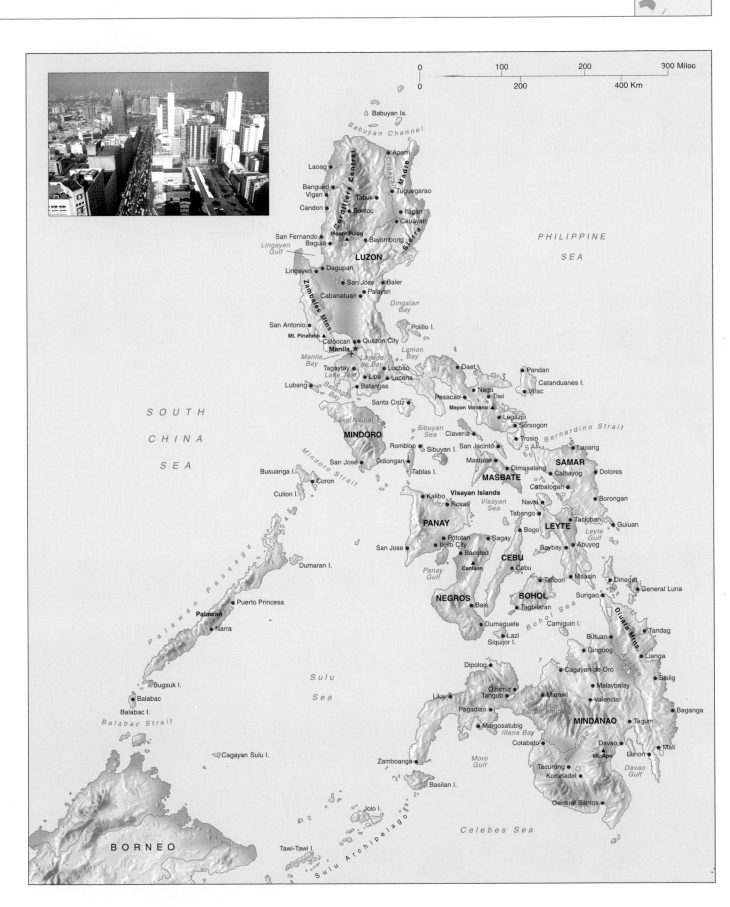

0   100   200   300 Miles
0   200   400 Km

Babuyan Is.

Babuyan Channel

Laoag ●
Aparri ●

Bangued ●
Vigan ●   Tabuk ●   Tuguegarao ●

Candon ●   Bontoc ●   Ilagan ●
Cauayan ●

San Fernando ●   Mount Pulog ▲
Baguio ●   Bayombong ●

Lingayen Gulf   **LUZON**

Lingayen ●   ● Dagupan
San Jose ●   Baler ●
Cabanatuan ●   Palayan ●

Dingalan Bay

San Antonio ●

Polillo I. ●
Mt. Pinatubo ▲   Caloocan ●   Quezon City ●
Manila ★   *Lamon Bay*

Manila Bay   *Laguna de Bay*
Tagaytay ●   Lucban ●   Daet ●   Pandan ●
Lubang ●   Lake Taal   Lipa ●   Lucena ●
Catanduanes I.
Batangas ●   Naga ●   Tiwi ●   Virac ●
Batangas Bay   Pasacao ●
Santa Cruz ●   Mayon Volcano ▲
Legazpi ●

SOUTH   Lake Naujan   Sorsogon ●
Trosin ●   *San Bernardino Strait*
CHINA   *Sibuyan Sea*   Claveria ●
MINDORO   Laoang ●
San Jacinto ●
SEA   Romblon ●   Sibuyan I.
Masbate ●
San José ●   Odiongan ●   Dimasalang ●   Calbayog ●   Dolores ●
Busuanga I.   Tablas I.   **MASBATE**   Catbalogan ●   **SAMAR**
Coron ●   **Visayan Islands**   Borongan ●
Culion I.   Kalibo ●   *Visayan Sea*   Naval ●
Roxas ●   Tabango ●   **LEYTE**   Tacloban ●   Guiuan ●
Leyte Gulf
PANAY   Bogo ●   Abuyog ●
Pototan ●   Sagay ●
Dumaran I.   San Jose ●   Iloilo City ●   Baybay ●
Bacolod ●   **CEBU**
Panay Gulf   Canlaon ▲   Cebu ●
Puerto Princesa ●   **NEGROS**   **BOHOL**   Tañbon ●   Maasin ●   Dinagat ●   General Luna ●
Palawan   Bais ●   Surigao ●
Narra ●   Tagbilaran ●
Dumaguete ●   *Bohol Sea*   Camiguin I.   **Diuata Mtns.**   Tandag ●
Lazi ●   Bûtuan ●   Lianga ●
Siquijor I.   Gingoog ●
Bugsuk I. ●   Dipolog ●   Cagayan de Oro ●   Bislig ●
Balabac ●   *Sulu*   Ozamiz ●   Malaybalay ●
Balabac I.   Tangub ●   Marawi ●   Valencia ●
Balabac Strait   *Sea*   Liloy ●   Lake Sultan Alonto   Baganga ●
Pagadian ●   **MINDANAO**
Margosatubig ●   Tagum ●
Illana Bay
Cagayan Sulu I.   Cotabato ●   Davao ●   Lupon ●   Mati ●
Zamboanga ●   *Moro Gulf*   Tacurong ●   ▲ Mt. Apo   *Davao Gulf*
Koronadel ●
Basilan I.   General Santos ●

BORNEO   Jolo I.
Sulu Archipelago   *Celebes Sea*
Tawi-Tawi I.

Palawan Passage

Mindoro Strait

Sulu Sea

PHILIPPINE SEA

Indesia

Status:	Republic
Area:	741,097 square miles
Population:	212 million
Capital:	Jakarta
Languages:	Bahasa Indonesia, Dutch, English
Currency:	Rupiah (100 sen)

Indonesia consists of more than 13,600 islands strung out in a 3,100-mile chain across a vast expanse of tropical sea between the eastern Indian Ocean and the western Pacific Ocean. Many of the islands cover only a few square miles, but Indonesia also includes some of the world's largest islands. Sumatra, for example, is nearly 1,060 miles long, and Java is more than 620 miles long. Indonesia also includes the western half of the world's second-largest island, New Guinea, called Irian Jaya, and more than three-quarters of the world's third-largest island, Borneo, which makes up the province of

Kalimantan. People inhabit about half the islands, but 80 percent of the population live on Sumatra, Java, Kalimantan, Sulawesi, and Irian Jaya, with almost half the total population crowded onto Java.

Most of Indonesia's people are of Malay descent, but the population also includes Chinese, Papuans, Arabs, and Polynesians. **Islam** is the dominant religion, but millions of people on the smaller islands and in remote inland regions also follow ancient traditional beliefs. The largest cities are the capital of Jakarta, Surabaya, and Bandung (all on Java) and Medan on Sumatra. The majority of the nation's people, however, live in small rural communities.

The Indonesian islands are dotted with hundreds of active volcanoes. Mountains covered in dense, **tropical rain forest** dominate the interior regions, while broad fertile plains fringe the coasts. Forestry workers extract teak, ebony, and other valuable hardwoods from the forests—chiefly on Borneo and Sumatra. Rattan and bamboo are also harvested for making mats and furniture. Most village houses are made of these versatile materials.

Agriculture is the backbone of Indonesia's economy. The country's farmers benefit from rich volcanic soil, plentiful rain, and year-round sunshine, all of which allows them to grow a wide variety of crops. Large plantations on the main islands produce coffee beans, tea, sugarcane, palm oil, rubber, and

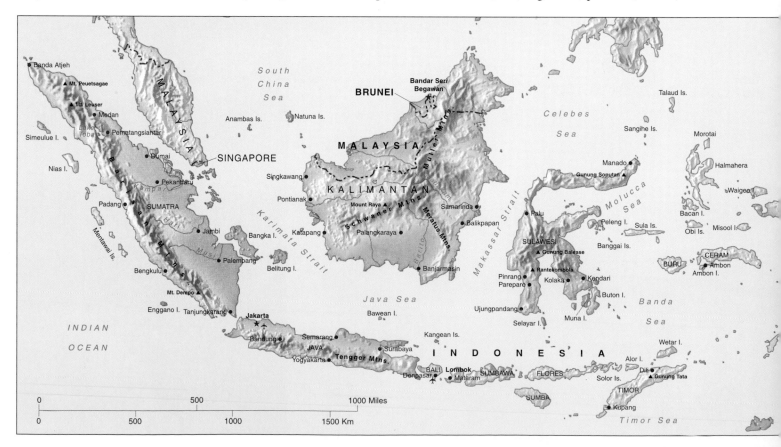

Above: Indonesian houses are built with several striking traditional designs. This style, built by the Minangkabau people of Sumatra, has roof ends that sweep upward like the horns of a water buffalo.

Below: Protected from the hot sun by a wide hat made of woven bamboo, a young Indonesian villager heads for the rice fields.

tobacco as cash crops. Smaller farms grow rice as their main food crop, along with maize, sweet potatoes, cassava, bananas, and other fruits and vegetables. Rural farms are not highly mechanized. Most farmers use traditional hand tools, and plows and carts are pulled by oxen and water buffalo. Many farmers also raise pigs, goats, and poultry for the table. In coastal areas, sardines, anchovies, tuna, prawns, and shellfish provide the protein in people's diets.

Oil and natural gas fields on Java and Sumatra supply fuel to the islands and are also Indonesia's principal export. Tin, from islands off the northern coast of Sumatra, is the country's second major mineral export. Miners also extract smaller amounts of coal, copper, manganese, and nickel. Manufacturing is a relatively small part of the economy and is concentrated almost entirely on Java. Factory workers process food products for export and make textiles, glassware, rubber products such as car tires, furniture, paper, and other wood products. Newer industries include car and truck assembly plants and petrochemical plants fed by the country's oil fields.

Malaysia, Singapore, Brunei

Malaysia

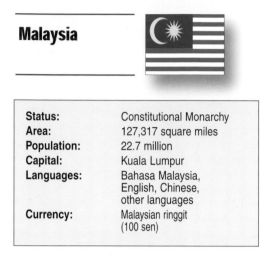

Status:	Constitutional Monarchy
Area:	127,317 square miles
Population:	22.7 million
Capital:	Kuala Lumpur
Languages:	Bahasa Malaysia, English, Chinese, other languages
Currency:	Malaysian ringgit (100 sen)

Malaysia has two large but widely separated land areas. West Malaysia consists of the southern end of the long, paddle-shaped Malay Peninsula that also holds Thailand. East Malaysia, 400 miles away across the South China Sea, consists of the territories of Sarawak and Sabah on the northern side of the island of Borneo. (The other parts of Borneo belong to Indonesia or form the independent country of Brunei.)

Malaysia was formed in 1963, when the **Federation** of Malaya and the British colonies of Singapore, Sarawak, and Sabah joined together. Singapore left the federation in 1965 to become an independent country.

Roughly 50 percent of the people of Malaysia are Malay, 35 percent are Chinese, and 10 percent are Indian. The rest, especially people in Sarawak and Sabah, belong to many smaller ethnic groups. This ethnic diversity gives Malaysia a rich and varied culture in which art, music, dance, drama, and sports play a part. Islam, **Hinduism, Buddhism,** and Christianity exist side by side without conflict.

Much of Malaysia is covered in dense tropical rain forests. From the Thai border, a ridge of mountains runs down the Malay Peninsula, where 80 percent of Malaysians live. The ridge forms a thinly populated inland zone that is separated from the densely populated coastal cities.

Rugged mountains dominate the interior of Sarawak and Sabah, while fertile plains line parts of the coast. The highlands of East Malaysia are famous for their dramatic limestone scenery. Towering rock outcrops loom out of the forest, and huge cave systems run for miles beneath the surface.

Above: Old architecture of the colonial period contrasts with Malaysia's modern building styles.

Malaysia's economy, one of the strongest in Asia, is based on agriculture, industry, and trade. The country produces half the world's palm oil and one-third of the world's rubber, as well as being a major supplier of cacao beans, tobacco, coconuts, tea, peppers, pineapples, and other fruits. Malaysia's forests yield valuable hardwoods that are shipped worldwide as logs, boards, veneers, plywood, and furniture. Malaysia is the world's third-largest producer of tin and ranks as a major producer of oil and gas. Long-established industries make textiles, rubber goods, timber products, and foodstuffs, while a host of new high-tech industries export electronic equipment, industrial chemicals, pharmaceuticals, and plastics, chiefly to Japan, Singapore, the United States, and Europe. This strong economic base gives most of Malaysia's people access to good educational and health-care services.

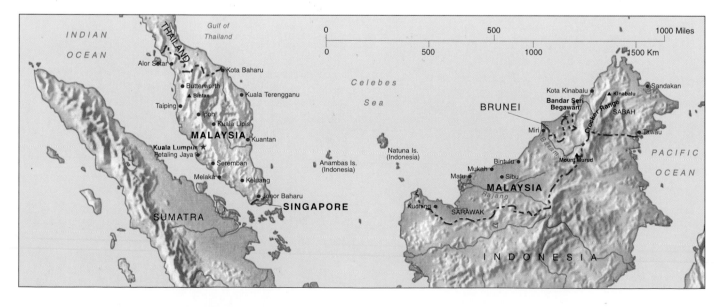

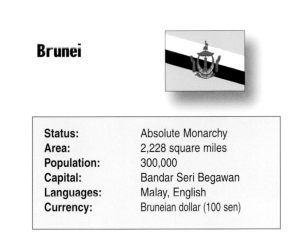

Singapore

Status:	Republic
Area:	239 square miles
Population:	4.0 million
Capital:	Singapore
Languages:	Malay, Mandarin Chinese, English, Tamil
Currency:	Singaporean dollar (100 cents)

Brunei

Status:	Absolute Monarchy
Area:	2,228 square miles
Population:	300,000
Capital:	Bandar Seri Begawan
Languages:	Malay, English
Currency:	Bruneian dollar (100 sen)

Singapore is a small country by area, but it is one of the economic powerhouses of Southeast Asia. The country consists of one main island (Singapore Island) and about 50 smaller ones that are clustered at the tip of the Malay Peninsula. The city of Singapore is the capital and one of the world's busiest seaports.

The skyline of the crowded, bustling capital is dominated by the high-rise towers of its commercial district. These structures rise above traditional shops, elegant apartment buildings, shopping malls, industrial districts, and the container terminals, warehouses, and repair yards that service the endless flow of ships.

Forests once covered Singapore's low-lying land, but most of the trees were cut down in colonial days to make way for groves of nutmeg, cloves, rubber, and coconuts. Almost half the land is built on, and most of the rest consists of parks and other public spaces. Singapore's small amount of farmland produces fruit and vegetables for local use, but most of the island's food has to be imported. Water is piped in from Malaysia to meet the city's needs.

Like Malaysia, Singapore has a diverse population. About 78 percent are Chinese, 14 percent Malay, and 7 percent Indian. A small number of Europeans and Americans live in Singapore, where hundreds of international companies have offices.

Singapore's wealth comes from importing and exporting goods from all over the world. It also has a thriving manufacturing sector making electrical and electronic goods, textiles, clothing, cameras, scientific instruments, chemicals, plastics, and food products. Heavy industry consists of ship repairs and oil refining.

The wealth generated by Singapore's economy provides the people with some of the highest living standards in Asia, including high wages, free schools, modern health-care services, and a rich cultural life. More than 90 percent of the people can read and write, one of the highest literacy rates in Asia.

Brunei is a small W-shaped country on the northern coast of the island of Borneo, facing the South China Sea. Most of the country consists of a broad coastal plain that rises inland to wooded hills. Formerly a British **protectorate,** Brunei achieved independence in 1984 and is ruled by a sultan (king) who is elected for life by a council of senior politicians. About 65 percent of the people are Malay and predominantly Muslim (followers of Islam). Another 25 percent are Chinese and Christian. More than 70 percent of the population live in the towns and cities.

The mainstays of Brunei's economy are the oil and gas fields that lie beneath its coastal waters. Money from the sale of oil and gas has made Brunei wealthy. The people enjoy a high standard of living, with free education and health care. The government is the country's largest employer, providing jobs for more than half the nation's workforce. The remainder work on small farms, in the coastal fisheries, and in small factories making consumer goods, chiefly for local use.

Right: Modern office blocks tower over Singapore's waterfront.

Vietnam, Laos, Cambodia

Vietnam

Status:	Republic
Area:	128,066 square miles
Population:	79.5 million
Capital:	Hanoi
Languages:	Vietnamese, French, English
Currency:	Dông (100 xu)

Vietnam is a long, narrow, S-shaped country with a 2,140-mile-long coastline on the South China Sea. The country stretches 1,030 miles north to south and 380 miles west to east at its widest, although the central section is barely 30 miles wide.

France controlled Vietnam before World War II, but Japan occupied the country during the war. France's efforts to regain control after the war were defeated in 1954 by the Communist army of the Vietminh. Peace negotiators divided the country into Communist North and non-Communist South, but fighting soon broke out between the two nations and escalated into a full-scale civil war. The United States was deeply involved in support of South Vietnam but withdrew when the two Vietnams declared a cease-fire in 1973. In 1975 the Communist regime unified the country.

Densely forested mountains cover northwestern Vietnam, continuing in a narrow mountain chain along the borders with Laos and Cambodia. Most Vietnamese live in two large river deltas that dominate eastern Vietnam. The Red River Delta in the north and the Mekong Delta in the south provide fertile farmland where Vietnamese farmers grow rice, corn, cassava, soybeans, vegetables, peanuts, coconuts, coffee beans, and cacao beans. Cotton, **jute,** rubber, and tobacco are the main nonfood crops. Fishing crews catch crabs, lobsters, shrimp, and squid off the coast. Apart from coal in the north, Vietnam has few mineral resources. Factory workers produce farm machinery, bicycles, cement, fertilizers, and textiles.

Laos

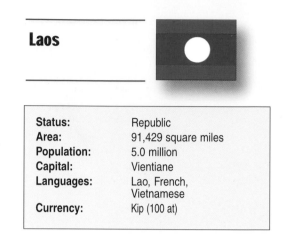

Status:	Republic
Area:	91,429 square miles
Population:	5.0 million
Capital:	Vientiane
Languages:	Lao, French, Vietnamese
Currency:	Kip (100 at)

Laos, like its neighbor Vietnam, was formerly a French-controlled territory. The country threw off foreign control in 1954 but then suffered a long period of civil war before it emerged as an independent Communist state in 1975.

Mountains blanketed in dense, humid tropical rain forest cover the north of the country, while broad, fertile lowlands along the Mekong River and its many tributaries dominate the south. Farmers in the highlands grow corn, rice, tobacco, and cotton. Lowland farmers harvest rice as their principal crop, along with vegetables, fruit, corn, and coffee beans. Most farmers also raise pigs, cattle, and poultry.

Laos is rich in natural resources but poor in infrastructure—the roads, refineries, and other operations that help export the resources. As a result, its deposits of gold, lead, silver, tin, zinc, and other minerals and its valuable stand of tropical hardwoods, gums, and resins have yet to be tapped.

Left: Vietnam's rivers provide a natural playground for young Vietnamese.

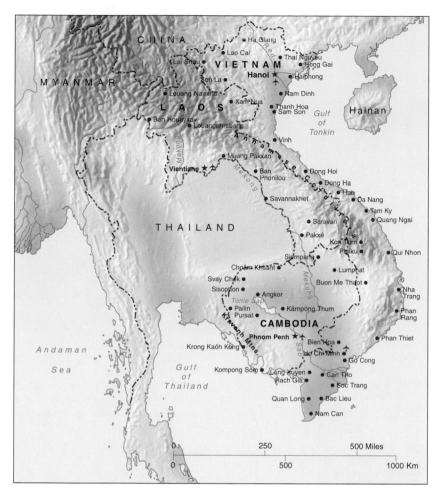

Cambodia

Status:	Constitutional Monarchy
Area:	69,900 square miles
Population:	11.9 million
Capital:	Phnom Penh
Languages:	Khmer, Chinese, Vietnamese, French
Currency:	Riel (100 sen)

Cambodia is a mainly lowland country in Southeast Asia, ringed by low forested hills along its borders with Thailand, Laos, and Vietnam. In the south, Cambodia has a short coast on the Gulf of Thailand. The country's principal port, Kompong Som, lies on the south side of a large enclosed bay, just over 100 miles southwest of the capital city of Phnom Penh.

The largest ethnic group in Cambodia is the Khmer, whose ancestors ruled a vast empire in Southeast Asia about a thousand years ago. The magnificent ruined temples of Angkor, capital of the Khmer Empire, are among the most spectacular ancient monuments in southern Asia.

In 1863, the tradition of royal rule gave way to French control as part of French Indochina. Cambodia became fully independent in 1954 but then suffered years of civil war. For nearly 20 years, it was ruled harshly by the Communist Khmer Rouge. In 1993 Cambodia's monarchy was reinstated.

Most of Cambodia's people are farmers, living in small lowland villages. With fertile soils, plentiful rain, and numerous rivers to provide water, most farmers grow two or even three crops of rice a year. Rivers, lakes, and warm offshore waters yield Cambodia's other main food—fish. Cotton and rubber are important commercial crops. Factory workers produce textiles, plywood, cement, and tires.

Left: Water buffalo are the "living tractors" of rural Asia. They pull carts and plows, haul logs in the forests, and drive threshers, water pumps, sugarcane presses, and other machines.

Myanmar and Thailand

Myanmar

Status:	Republic
Area:	261,228 square miles
Population:	48.1 million
Capital:	Yangon
Languages:	Burmese, English, several local dialects
Currency:	Kyat (100 pyas)

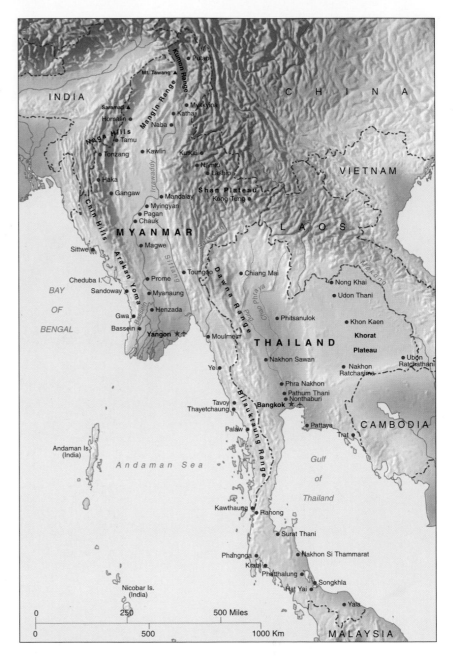

Myanmar has a 1,650-mile-long coastline on the Bay of Bengal and shares its land borders with Bangladesh, India, China, Laos, and Thailand. The country changed its name from Burma in 1989, but many Burmese who oppose the government still use the old name.

Myanmar is a land of mountains, dense tropical rain forests, and great river valleys. The low-lying Arakan Yoma range in the west overlooks a narrow fertile plain fronting the Bay of Bengal. This highland region runs northward through the Chin and Naga Hills along Myanmar's border with India. Clothed in tropical forests, the hills hold much of the world's teak—one of Myanmar's most valuable exports. The high peaks of the Kumon range—rising to 19,296-foot Hkakabo Razi in the far north—and the Shan Plateau's wooded hills separate Myanmar from China. To the east, the Tanen and Dawna Mountains dominate the country's borders with Thailand and Laos.

Three great rivers—the Irrawaddy, the Sittang, and the Salween—and their tributaries flow from north to south through Myanmar's middle. Low-lying hills separate the rivers from one another. Their broad, fertile valleys support the country's most productive farmland. The many mouths of the Irrawaddy spill into the Bay of Bengal through a huge delta. To the east of the delta, the Sittang and the Salween empty into the Andaman Sea. The capital city of Yangon (formerly called Rangoon) and several other towns and cities are built in the delta area. Other towns lie along the coast or inland in the principal river valleys.

About 75 percent of Myanmar's people live in small villages of thatched bamboo houses. Some of the homes sit on stilts to protect against river floods brought on by the monsoon rains. Myanmar's economy is still developing, but nearly 80 percent of Burmese can read and write, many attend college, and most have better health care than people do in other developing Asian countries.

More than 60 percent of Myanmar's workforce tends the soil. Rice is the principal crop—covering more than half the cultivated land—supplemented by fruits and vegetables, sugarcane, wheat, tobacco, cotton, and rubber. Factories concentrated in Yangon manufacture textiles, metal wares, and processed foods. Forestry and fishing are also significant employers. Myanmar has large reserves of undeveloped mineral wealth and is a major producer of jade, rubies, and sapphires, which are exported worldwide.

Thailand

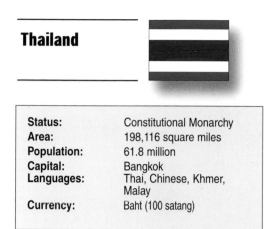

Status:	Constitutional Monarchy
Area:	198,116 square miles
Population:	61.8 million
Capital:	Bangkok
Languages:	Thai, Chinese, Khmer, Malay
Currency:	Baht (100 satang)

Thailand is a tropical Southeast Asian country of forests, mountains, lakes, and rivers. Winters are mild, springtime is hot and dry, and summers are long, hot, and very humid. The climate is generally hot and sticky along the coasts but cooler and drier in the northern highlands.

About 75 percent of Thailand's people live in rural areas. Farming is the principal occupation, and rice is the dominant crop. Farmers also cultivate cassava, corn, soybeans, sugarcane, bananas, coconuts, and pineapples. Cotton, jute, and rubber are the chief nonfood crops.

Thailand also has considerable mineral wealth. Miners dig up zinc, copper, feldspar, kaolin, lead, limestone, and lignite. Buried in the sandbars of Thailand's shallow coastal waters are some of the world's richest tin deposits—making Thailand one of the world's leading suppliers of that valuable mineral. The country extracts natural gas from offshore wells in the Gulf of Thailand but otherwise is short of fuel and has to import most of the oil it needs.

Tropical hardwoods—especially teak—were one of Thailand's chief exports until unregulated cutting created mudslides, rock falls, and massive soil erosion. Enormous environmental damage and destruction of entire villages led the Thai government to halt hardwood cutting in 1988. The country focused on developing other industries, especially tourism and manufacturing. The capital city of Bangkok has become a major manufacturing center, producing textiles, automobiles, electronic goods, cement, pharmaceuticals, paper, plywood, and agricultural chemicals.

Thailand's growing economy supports free primary schools and a large number of secondary schools and colleges. Nearly 90 percent of the population can read and write. But the drift of poor rural people to the cities and the continued presence of many Vietnamese refugees have placed great pressure on housing and other services.

Top: More than 400 temples grace Thailand's capital, Bangkok, on the delta of the Chao Phraya River. Their intricately decorated walls and ornate spires are a major tourist attraction.

Above left: The Golden Temple near the capital Yangon in southern Myanmar

Above right: Traders and shoppers throng the floating markets of Bangkok's rivers and canals.

India

Status:	Federal Republic
Area:	1,269,340 square miles
Population:	986.6 million
Capital:	New Delhi
Languages:	Hindi, English, Telugu, Bengali, Marathi, Urdu, other regional dialects
Currency:	Indian rupee (100 paisa)

India is the world's seventh-largest country but is second only to China in population. Nearly one billion people—one-sixth of the world's people—live in India.

Long before humans lived there, the Indian **subcontinent** had a remarkable and spectacular history. Along with South America, Africa, Antarctica, and Australia, India once formed part of a vast supercontinent, called Gondwana, that was situated much farther south of its current location. When Gondwana broke apart more than 200 million years ago, India drifted northward, crossed the equator, and crashed into the landmass that would become Asia.

The collision didn't happen quickly, like a car wreck. It took millions of years. But India plowed so hard into Asia that it buckled and crushed a 1,500-mile long, 200-mile-wide section of the earth's crust, pushing it five miles into the sky. The result of that geological collision is the Himalayas—the world's tallest mountain range, which marks India's borders with China, Nepal, and Bhutan.

The huge diamond-shaped sub-continent—2,000 miles from north to south and 1,000 miles across at its widest—contains enough variety of landscapes and people to be several countries. Snow-covered mountain peaks and vast open plains meet deserts, high plateaus, and dense rain forests.

Left: Houses, temples, boats, and people crowd every inch of the Ganges riverfront at Varanasi in the north central Indian state of Uttar Pradesh. To Hindus, the Ganges is the most sacred river in India.

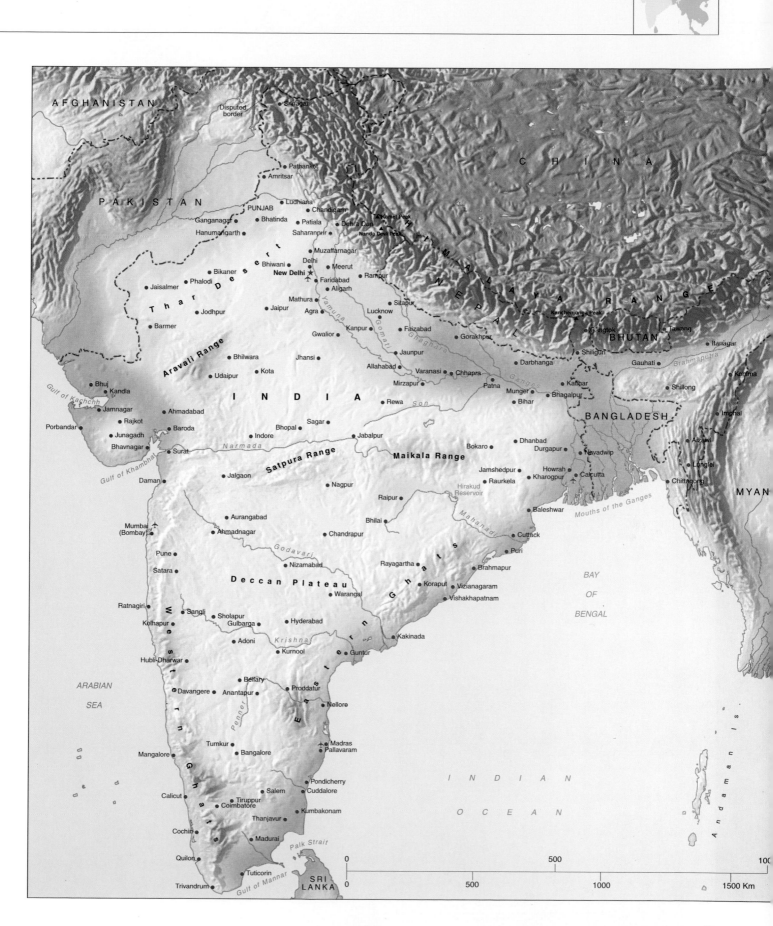

AFGHANISTAN

Disputed
border

Srinagar

CHINA

PAKISTAN

Pathankot

Amritsar

PUNJAB

Ludhiana

Chandigarh

Ganganagar

Bhatinda

Patiala

Dehra Dun

Kamet Peak

Hanumangarth

Saharanpur

Nanda Devi Peak

Muzaffarnagar

NEPAL

Bikaner

Bhiwani

Delhi

Meerut

Kanchenjunga Peak

Phalodi

New Delhi

Faridabad

Rampur

Gangtok

BHUTAN

Jaisalmer

Mathura

Aligarh

Tawang

Jodhpur

Jaipur

Agra

Sitapur

Itanagar

Barmer

Lucknow

Kanpur

Faizabad

Gorakhpur

Shiliguri

Gauhati

Brahmaputra

Bhilwara

Jhansi

Gwalior

Jaunpur

Darbhanga

Kohima

Udaipur

Kota

Allahabad

Varanasi

Chhapra

Ganges

Katihar

Shillong

Bhuj

Kandla

Mirzapur

Patna

Munger

Bhagalpur

Jamnagar

Rajkot

Ahmadabad

INDIA

Rewa

Son

Bihar

BANGLADESH

Imphal

Porbandar

Junagadh

Baroda

Bhopal

Sagar

Indore

Jabalpur

Bokaro

Dhanbad

Durgapur

Navadwip

Aizawl

Bhavnagar

Surat

Narmada

Maikala Range

Jamshedpur

Howrah

Calcutta

Lunglei

Daman

Jalgaon

Satpura Range

Nagpur

Raurkela

Kharogpur

Chittagong

MYAN

Mumbai
(Bombay)

Aurangabad

Ahmadnagar

Chandrapur

Raipur

Bhilai

Hirakud
Reservoir

Baleshwar

Cuttack

Mouths of the Ganges

Pune

Godavari

Nizamabad

Rayagartha

Brahmapur

Puri

BAY

Satara

Deccan Plateau

Warangal

Korapur

Vizianagaram

Vishakhapatnam

OF

BENGAL

Ratnagiri

Sangli

Sholapur

Hyderabad

Kolhapur

Gulbarga

Krishna

Adoni

Kurnool

Guntur

Kakinada

Hubli-Dharwar

ARABIAN

SEA

Bellary

Proddatur

Davangere

Anantapur

Nellore

Penner

Tumkur

Madras

Mangalore

Bangalore

Pallavaram

INDIAN

OCEAN

Andaman Is.

Calicut

Salem

Pondicherry

Cuddalore

Tiruppur

Coimbatore

Kumbakonam

Thanjavur

Cochin

Madurai

Quilon

Palk Strait

Tuticorin

Trivandrum

Gulf of Mannar

SRI
LANKA

0   500   100

0   500   1000   1500 Km

India

India's people speak 14 major languages and more than 1,000 additional languages and dialects. About one-third of the population principally speaks Hindi—one of India's 14 official languages. Millions more use it as their second language. English, a reminder of India's colonial connection to Britain, is still widely used in government circles and by the legal, academic, and scientific communities.

India was home to two very early civilizations—one centered in the Indus Valley around 2600 B.C., the other in the Ganges Valley around 1500 B.C. Over the centuries, India has been both a large sprawling empire and a collection of separate states. Colonists from Portugal, Britain, France, and the Netherlands arrived in the fifteenth and sixteenth centuries, but the **British East India Company** steadily established itself as the dominant power. The British government formally colonized India in 1805, and it remained under British rule until 1947. At that time, India was divided, or partitioned, into modern India, which is predominantly Hindu, and the primarily Muslim state of Pakistan. Border conflicts between the two states and religious conflicts both between the states and within each state have plagued the subcontinent ever since.

India can be divided into three major land regions. In the north is a strip of foothills and the towering peaks of the Himalayas, which hold India's highest summit, Kanchen-junga, (28,208 feet). Few people live in the high mountains, but villagers in the foothills graze sheep and goats on the mountain pastures and grow rice, wheat, and vegetables. Farmers in northern India grow rice on the fertile soil of the terraced foothills and cultivate fruit and nut trees. Above the terraces, the dry, rugged hills are crossed by ancient tracks that lead northward into China and westward into Pakistan. Far to the east, where India borders Myanmar, greater rainfall allows upland farmers to raise wheat, barley, and rice. Parts of this region enjoy more than 300 inches of annual rain. The village of Cherrapunji holds the world record for a single year's rainfall—1,042 inches. Forests throughout the foothills provide construction timber and fuel for

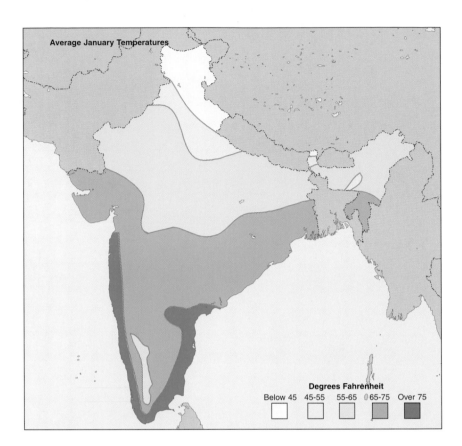

Average January Temperatures

Degrees Fahrenheit

Below 45   45-55   55-65   65-75   Over 75

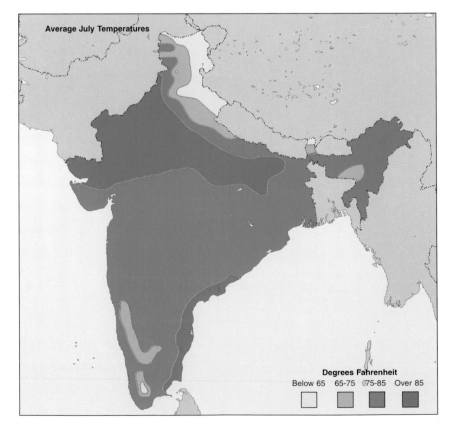

Average July Temperatures

Degrees Fahrenheit

Below 65   65-75   75-85   Over 85

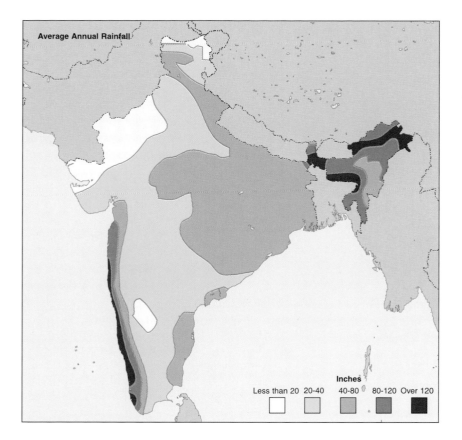

Average Annual Rainfall

Inches

Less than 20 | 20-40 | 40-80 | 80-120 | Over 120

Left and above: From October to March, dry winter **monsoon** winds bring cool air to northern India from Asia. Southern India remains hot throughout the year. From April to June—the hot season—temperatures on the northern plains often exceed 100˚F. June to October is the summer monsoon, when warm, moist winds from the Indian Ocean bring heavy rain, especially to the western coast and northeastern India.

homes, but in many areas too much wood has been cut and the hillsides are badly eroded.

South of the mountains, a broad plain stretches from east to west across the continent, ending in the hot and dusty Thar Desert. Only small groups of sheep and goat herders roamed the desert until 1986, when a new canal provided irrigation for crops and farmers were encouraged to settle there. The desert also contains one of India's nuclear power stations and the country's nuclear test site.

The tropical state of Gujarat, south of the desert and bordering the Arabian Sea, is one of India's principal cotton-growing regions. The country's great rivers—the Ganges and the Brahmaputra—dominate the central and eastern plains. Fed by runoff from Himalayan glaciers and snowfields, the rivers and their tributaries flow across broad fertile plains, meeting in Bangladesh before emptying into the Bay of Bengal. The rivers provide ample irrigation, allowing the plains' farmers to grow much of India's food. Rice covers the greatest percentage of India's cultivated land, but farmers also raise wheat, millet, sorghum, and

many varieties of peas and beans. Local markets also brim with onions, cauliflower, eggplant, potatoes, apples, and bananas. Many farmers harvest and sell tea, sugarcane, cotton, jute, tobacco, and rubber.

Farther south lies India's great triangular Deccan Peninsula, a huge plateau sloping gently from west to east. Rocky mountain ranges mark the plateau's edge. The steep, 5,000-foot Western Ghats overlook a narrow coastal plain on the Arabian Sea, while the 2,000-foot Eastern Ghats slope to a broader coastal plain facing the Bay of Bengal. On most of the Deccan, farmers grow grains and vegetables, and they raise large herds of cattle and buffalo. Western Deccan farmers take advantage of their wetter soil to plant mainly cotton and sorghum. Farmers in the drier eastern sector harvest millet, beans, sugarcane, and spices.

India's southwestern coast enjoys a hot tropical climate with more than 120 inches of annual rain and abundant crops of peppers, mangoes, bananas, and coconuts. Coastal inhabitants eat a great deal of fish, supporting a large portion of India's fishing industry. Vessels come home bursting with prawns, mackerel, herring, sardines, shark, and Bombay duck—a small fish that is dried and used in many curried dishes.

About 70 percent of India's people reside in small farming communities, often numbering no more than 1,000 people. The remaining 30 percent live in towns and small cities. Only about 250 urban areas house more than 100,000 people, and just 10 of them have more than a million people—the three largest being Calcutta (11 million), Mumbai (formerly Bombay, 10 million), and Delhi (7 million). But the urban population is growing quickly, as the rural poor flock to urban areas in search of jobs.

Although India's major cities are among the most crowded urban environments in the world, recent government health and education programs have had considerable success. Since the 1950s, life expectancy has increased by 25 years, as new hospitals and clinics have been built. Teams of health workers have visited thousands of rural communities giving advice on childcare, nutrition, hygiene, and sanitation.

India

Above: The people of rural India depend on oxen, bullocks, and buffalo for transportation.

Below: The scenery of northern India includes dramatic mountain passes.

The government has also invested in schools, teachers, books, and public television services, all of which have led to a dramatic rise in India's literacy rate. About half the population can read and write—more than twice as many as in the 1950s, when these programs began.

Agricultural progress has not been as dramatic. Parts of the northwest are very dry and have suffered severe droughts. The rest of the country lies at the heart of the Asian monsoon region. From June to October, warm winds blow in from the southwest carrying moisture from the Indian Ocean. This moisture falls as torrential rain and often causes flooding in low-lying areas like the Ganges Delta. The Bay of Bengal is also prone to hurricanes.

India's industries have grown rapidly since independence. More people are employed in the textile industries than in any other sector. Mumbai and Ahmadabad in the west are the principal cotton centers, wool processing is based in Punjab in the far northwest, and jute factories are concentrated around Calcutta.

Above: A camel driver, from the state of Rajasthan in western India

Above right: A typical scene of daily life at Madurai in southern India

Right: A farmer heads for the local market in Tamil Nadu, a state in southeastern India.

Textiles and clothing are among India's principal exports. Iron and steel plants at Bhilai, Bokaro, Durgapur, and Raurkela in the eastern Deccan process local iron ore with locally mined coal to supply steel for factory-made cars, bicycles, railroad parts, household appliances, and other metal goods. Factory workers in cities such as Delhi, Ahmadabad, and Hyderabad manufacture electrical goods, lace, decorative wood and leather goods, fine brassware, and food products for both local and overseas markets. India's chemical plants produce pharmaceuticals, dyes, fertilizers, and industrial chemicals. India meets more than half its energy needs with local resources. Power stations burn Deccan coal and use oil from wells off the coast near Mumbai and onshore in Assam. Another 35 percent is hydroelectric power from major river stations, and the remainder is nuclear power.

Bangladesh, Sri Lanka, Maldives

Bangladesh

Status:	Republic
Area:	55,598 square miles
Population:	125.7 million
Capital:	Dhaka
Languages:	Bengali, English
Currency:	Taka
	(100 poisha)

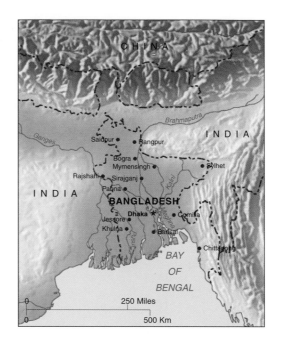

Bangladesh consists almost entirely of a flat alluvial plain, formed over millions of years by the meandering and frequent flooding of the country's three major rivers—the Ganges, the Brahmaputra, and the Meghna. They flow through Bangladesh to the Bay of Bengal. Most of the country lies less than 50 feet above sea level, making Bangladesh extremely prone to flooding. Heavy monsoon rains from June to October often cause the rivers to burst their banks, and cyclones sweeping in from the Bay of Bengal can drive enormous volumes of water inland. These awesome storms have devastated entire villages and left hundreds of square miles of crops rotting under several feet of muddy saltwater.

Bangladesh is one of the world's most heavily populated countries, with more than 2,200 people per square mile. It is also a very poor country. More than 80 percent of Bangladeshis live in rural areas and grow rice, wheat, beans, vegetables, and jute—the primary nonfood crop. The soil is fertile, and the government has made efforts to improve farm yields with fertilizers, better varieties of seed, and more modern farming methods. But with so many mouths to feed, most Bangladeshis do not have enough to eat.

Typical rural homes are built of bamboo and thatch. Only a third have electricity, running water, or sanitation. The cities are bursting, with millions of people living in makeshift homes in sprawling shantytowns. Health and educational services do not begin to meet the country's needs.

Jute factories—Bangladesh's only large-scale industrial employers—process the plant's fiber into ropes and sacking. Workers in small factories fabricate leather goods, textiles, pottery, and metal goods. Fishing boats that ply the coasts and rivers provide an important source of food, allowing Bangladesh to export large quantities of shrimp and prawns.

Opposite: Elephants are still widely used to haul logs in the forests. Handlers reward these strong, intelligent animals with a refreshing scrub in the river after a hard day.

Below: Bangladeshi school-children pose with their teacher. These children are lucky to attend school, as lack of money hampers the country's educational services.

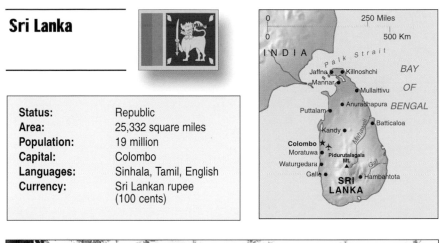

Sri Lanka

Status:	Republic
Area:	25,332 square miles
Population:	19 million
Capital:	Colombo
Languages:	Sinhala, Tamil, English
Currency:	Sri Lankan rupee (100 cents)

Droplet-shaped Sri Lanka is a beautiful island of wild animals, coastal plains, and forested mountains reaching up to 8,000 feet in the south. Once a British colony named Ceylon, the island is famous for its Ceylon tea, which it exports and consumes locally in great quantities.

Two major ethnic groups dominate life and politics in Sri Lanka. The mostly Buddhist Sinhalese comprise 74 percent of the population and largely control the government. The predominantly Hindu Tamil make up 18 percent of the country's inhabitants and feel their lack of political power has led to fewer educational and employment opportunities. Outbreaks of fighting between the rivals have plagued the island for nearly 50 years.

Sri Lanka's economy is based on farming. About half the labor force works the land, growing rice, rubber, tobacco, coconuts, and tea—Sri Lanka's most valuable export. Another 10 percent work in processing plants or textile factories. And the country's service industries—government offices, communications, and transportation—employ 35 percent. Colombo, on the southwestern coast, is the island's capital, largest city, and principal seaport.

Maldives

Status:	Republic
Area:	116 square miles
Population:	300,000
Capital:	Malé
Language:	Dhiyehi
Currency:	Rufiyaa (100 laari)

More than 1,000 coral islands make up the Maldives. They stretch in a 475-mile-long chain in the Indian Ocean. One of the world's smallest countries, the island group sits off India's southwestern tip, covering little more than 100 square miles. Just over 200 of the islands are inhabited. Many are tiny atolls that barely break the ocean surface. Some of the islands lie so low in the water that ocean experts fear they eventually may submerge altogether.

Maldivian livelihoods depend on fishing, tourism, and farming. Thousands of boats head to sea each day, pulling in bonito and tuna for local consumption and for export—primarily to Sri Lanka and Japan. Glistening white beaches and a hot, sunny tropical climate attract large numbers of visitors each year. Tourism is responsible for about 20 percent of the country's economy. Farmers on the islands grow crops—primarily millet, sweet potatoes, peppers, breadfruit, and other fruits—for local dinner tables and for the island's hotels.

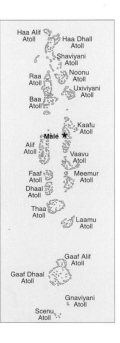

Nepal and Bhutan

Nepal

Status:	Constitutional Monarchy
Area:	56,826 square miles
Population:	24.3 million
Capital:	Kathmandu
Languages:	Nepali, many local dialects
Currency:	Nepalese rupee (100 paisa)

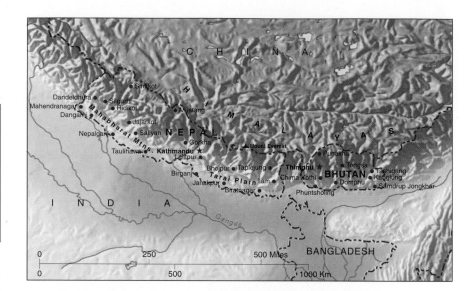

The remote mountain kingdom of Nepal lies in the Himalayas, sandwiched between China and India. More than 80 percent of the country is covered by these towering mountains the highest of which is Mount Everest (29,028 feet), and by the hills and valleys of a lesser range, the Mahabharat Mountains, that lies to the south. The broad fertile Tarai Plain stretches west to east across the southern edge of the country.

Nepal's mountainous terrain and lack of roads make communication difficult, especially for the 55 percent of the population that lives in the mountain regions. The economy is underdeveloped, and there are few schools or hospitals. A government program begun in the 1950s to improve health and educational services has raised the country's literacy rate from 5 percent to about 20 percent of the population, but lack of education remains one of Nepal's greatest barriers to progress.

Nearly all of the Nepalese depend on agriculture for their income. People in the high mountains raise sheep and longhaired yaks. The animals' milk is a fundamental part of the local diet, and their wool is woven to make clothes and blankets. Some crops in this area cling to the terraced hillsides, but much of the original forest has been cut for firewood, causing the hillsides to wash away. Farmers at the lower elevations benefit from better soils, a mild, cool climate, and summer rains. They harvest rice, corn, millet, wheat, and vegetables and

Above: Mount Everest, the world's tallest peak, stands on the border between Nepal and China.

herd cattle, oxen, sheep, and goats. Most Nepalese farmers work small family plots and manage to produce just enough food for their own needs, with a small surplus to sell or trade. Popular imports include kerosene and salt.

The Tarai Plain enjoys a hot, wet climate, with ample moisture and fertile soil. Farmers grow grains, vegetables, sugarcane, and nonfood crops such as jute and tobacco. Some sections of the Tarai are covered in jungles and swamps that are teeming with wildlife, such as crocodiles, elephants, leopards, rhinoceroses, and tigers.

Nepal's mineral resources—coal, iron, copper, and gold—are undeveloped because of their remote locations. The country has little industry apart from crafts, but countries such as the United States, Britain, Switzerland, and China are providing aid to create more industry and jobs. Nepal's hope for the future lies in its huge potential for hydroelectric power from Himalayan rivers. With international funding, Nepal will be able to build several giant power stations and to sell the electricity to the industrial regions of northern India.

Bhutan

Status:	Absolute Monarchy
Area:	18,147 square miles
Population:	800,000
Capital:	Thimphu
Languages:	Dzongkha, English
Currency:	Ngultrum (100 chetrum)

The tiny mountain kingdom of Bhutan lies between India and Tibet (formerly an independent country but since the 1950s a self-governing region of China). Like neighboring Nepal, Bhutan has three major land regions. The high Himalayas of the north are cold and windy, with ice-covered peaks and large areas of bare rock. Herders raise goats and yaks on the rough, windswept mountain pastures. South of the Himalayas, the land consists of low mountains and rolling hills that are densely covered with ash, oak, and poplars. Good soils and the milder, damper climate of the sheltered valleys allow farmers to grow wheat, barley, rice, and vegetables. Some of the lower south-facing hills are hot and humid, and the same climate pattern extends across the rolling plains and broad river valleys that cover the south of the country. Farmers in this fertile area grow rice, bananas, and citrus fruits, and miners in the south produce coal, much of which Bhutan exports to India.

With aid from India, Bhutan is modernizing its road system, improving its agriculture, and developing export industries such as food processing. A hydroelectric power station has been built to supply the capital, Thimphu, and others are planned.

Top: While chatting with friends at the local store, Nepalese men drink tea.

Above: Terraced rice paddies at Kanglung in eastern Bhutan

Right: A young Buddhist monk collects alms (donations, usually of food or drink) in the streets of his village. Most young Bhutanese men spend at least two years in a monastery.

Pakistan and Afghanistan

Pakistan

Status:	Federal Republic
Area:	307,375 square miles
Population:	146.5 million
Capital:	Islamabad
Languages:	Punjabi, Urdu, Sindhi, Pashtun, Baluchi, English
Currency:	Pakistan rupee (100 paisa)

Pakistan emerged as a country in 1947, when India gained its independence from Britain. A large section of the Indian subcontinent became the predominantly Hindu state of India. The other, smaller section became the Islamic state of Pakistan, home to a population that was 95 percent Muslim. Pakistan then consisted of West Pakistan and East Pakistan, two Muslim territories that were located nearly 1,000 miles apart. Civil war led to a breakup in 1971, and East Pakistan gained independence as Bangladesh. West Pakistan became simply Pakistan.

The dry, barren Baluchistan Plateau blankets most of southwestern Pakistan. With less than five inches of annual rainfall, the area supports little vegetation. Few people inhabit the region apart from scattered settlements of sheep and goat herders. In northern Pakistan, the land rises to the rugged mountains of the North-West Frontier Province, where the Khyber Pass links Pakistan with neighboring Afghanistan. Farther east rises the world's second-highest peak, K2 (also known as Godwin Austen), which towers 28,250 feet on the Himalayan border with China.

Stretching northward and eastward from the Arabian Sea, the Thar Desert reaches deep into India along several river valleys. Farmers have been able to tap into the area's rivers to irrigate parts of the desert for cultivation. The lowlands of the Indus River and its principal tributaries dominate Punjab and Sind Provinces of eastern Pakistan. Over millions of years, these rivers have deposited thick layers of silt, forming a broad, fertile **alluvial plain.** Even here, in Pakistan's wettest region, annual rainfall rarely exceeds 20 inches. The farmers of these plains channel the rivers into extensive irrigation systems, which allow the farmers to grow wheat, rice, chickpeas, vegetables, and fruits. Cotton and sugarcane are the country's primary nonfood crops.

Most of Pakistan is underdeveloped. Two-thirds of the people live in farming villages with few modern amenities. The country is short on schools and teachers, as well as on hospitals and medical staff. Despite government efforts to improve educational standards, less than 50 percent of school-age children attend classes, and only about one in four Pakistanis can read and write.

Manufacturing employs about 15 percent of the population, mostly in the urban centers of Karachi, Hyderabad, Lahore, Multan, Rawalpindi, and Peshawar. Factory workers produce textiles and clothing, processed foods, fertilizers, and cement. Along the coast, many Pakistanis work in the fishing industry, catching shrimp, sardines, shark, and other fish for local and foreign markets.

Below: A swaying suspension bridge spans a mountain river at Gilgit in the wild terrain of northeastern Pakistan.

Afghanistan

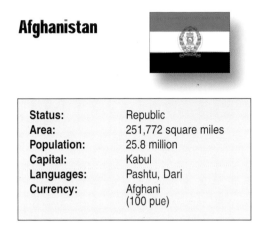

Status:	Republic
Area:	251,772 square miles
Population:	25.8 million
Capital:	Kabul
Languages:	Pashtu, Dari
Currency:	Afghani (100 pue)

Afghanistan is a rugged, mountainous, landlocked country ringed by Iran, Turkmenistan, Uzbekistan, Tajikistan, China, and Pakistan. Its people belong to more than 20 ethnic groups, and power struggles among them have led to constant political unrest. A military coup in 1973 replaced Afghanistan's monarchy with a republic, but further unrest led to occupation by Soviet troops. Since the Soviet withdrawal, internal conflicts have continued, and some have been extremely violent and disruptive.

Rolling plains and plateaus stretch across northern Afghanistan, supporting sheep and goat herders on sparse grasslands. The soil is fertile, but annual rainfall rarely exceeds seven inches. Farmers cultivate the river valleys, diverting water to their fields through irrigation channels. To assist the agricultural sector, the government has built large irrigation systems along some of the major rivers—the Helmand, the Qonduz, and the Harirud.

The high mountains of the Hindu Kush fill central Afghanistan, rising to more than 20,000 feet near the Pakistani border. Many Afghans live in the high, cold valleys of this region. The farmers grow grain and vegetables using hand tools and centuries-old farming methods, and they graze livestock on the sparse hillside pastures.

Arid plains and deserts cover southwestern Afghanistan. Rivers crossing this desolate western region flow into the Sistan Basin—an area of shallow salty lakes and marshlands. Farmers redirect the waters of the Helmand River to irrigate their fields of wheat, corn, and barley.

Afghanistan has little industry, and most of its rich mineral deposits lie undeveloped because of their remote locations. The country has developed two valuable minerals for export—natural gas and the stone lapis lazuli. Other exports include cotton, nuts, leather goods, silverware, jewelry, and the fine wool of the Karakul sheep.

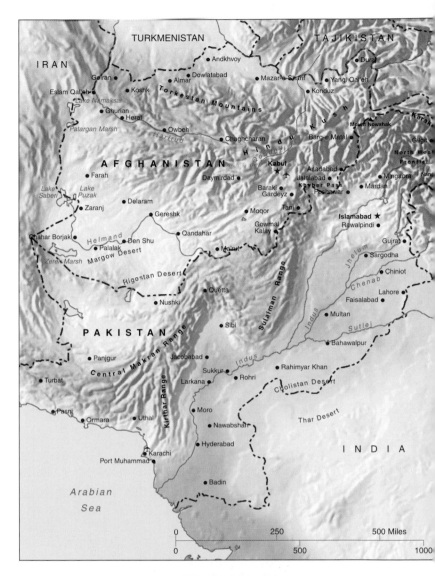

Above: A trekker takes a break amid the magnificent scenery of northeastern Afghanistan.

Glossary

alluvial plain: a level tract of land bordering a river on which sediment has been deposited

British East India Company: a private organization that opened trade with India and eastern Asia in the 1600s and that received special trading rights from the British government

Buddhism: a religion of Asia founded by Buddha. It teaches that through living a good life a person's soul is freed from pain, sorrow, and desire.

colony: a territory ruled by another country that is typically located far away

Communist: a person who supports Communism—an economic system in which the government owns all farmland and the means of producing goods in factories

delta: a triangular piece of land at the mouth of a river

federation: a form of government in which states or groups unite under a central power. The states or groups surrender power to make some decisions but retain limited territorial control.

glacier: a large body of ice and snow that moves slowly over land

hemp: a tall plant with tough fibers that can be made into rope and heavy cloth

Hinduism: the main religion of India. It emphasizes performing one's duty, especially through the observance of certain rituals and social obligations.

Islam: the religion of the world's Muslims. It emphasizes belief in Allah and in Muhammad as his prophet.

jute: a strong fiber that comes from plants that originated in eastern India. The fiber can be manufactured into twine and burlap sacking.

kapok: the silky fibers around the seeds of the tropical ceiba tree. The fibers are used to stuff mattresses, sleeping bags, and life preservers and as insulation.

loess: a yellowish glacial soil that is good for growing crops. The soil lies on the land and, during dry, windy times, is blown into the air.

monsoon: a rain-bearing wind that blows from the southwest in southern Asia roughly during the months of April to October

plateau: a large, relatively flat area that stands above the surrounding land

protectorate: a territory under the authority of another

seiner: a fishing vessel that pulls a large net, call a seine, that encloses fish in a vertical trap

steppe: a level, treeless plain

subcontinent: a large landmass that is a smaller but major division of a continent

subsistence farmer: a farmer who grows only enough food to feed the family, with little if any surplus for market

terrace: a flat platform of soil with sloping banks. A series of terraced fields, rising one above the other, can offer farmers more land for growing crops.

tropical rain forest: a dense, green forest that receives large amounts of rain every year. These forests lie near the equator.

Tropic of Cancer: an imaginary circle around the earth that parallels the equator to the north. The Tropic of Capricorn parallels the equator to the south. The hot, humid area between the two circles is called the tropics.

Index

A

Afghanistan, 45

B

Bangladesh, 6, 32, 40
Bhutan, 34, 42-43
Brunei, 28-29
Burma. *See* Myanmar

C

Cambodia, 30, 31
China, 6, 8-14, 16, 18, 32, 34, 42, 45;
    brief history of, 13, 14

E

earthquakes, 20
Everest, Mount, 6, 8, 42

G

Ganges River, 6, 34, 37, 40
Gobi Desert, 8, 16

H

Himalayas, 6, 34, 36, 42, 43, 44
Hong Kong, 6, 14

I

India, 6, 32, 34-39, 42, 43;
    brief history of, 36
Indonesia, 6, 26-27, 28
Islam, 26, 28, 29, 44

J

Japan, 6, 13, 20-23, 28, 41

L

Laos, 30-31, 32

M

Macao, 14
Malaysia, 28, 29
Maldives, 41
Mongolia, 6, 16-17
Myanmar, 32, 33

N

Nepal, 34, 42
North Korea, 18-19, 20

P

Pacific Ocean, 6, 10, 13, 22, 24, 26
Pakistan, 6, 36, 44-45
Philippines, 6, 24-25

R

Russia, 6, 20

S

Singapore, 6, 28-29
southern and eastern Asia, industries
    of, 6, 12, 14, 15, 17, 19, 22-23, 24,
    27, 28, 29, 32, 33, 39, 40, 42
southern and eastern Asia, land use in,
    6, 10, 11, 15, 16-17, 19, 22-23, 24,
    26-27, 28, 29, 30, 31, 33, 36-37,
    42, 43, 44, 45
southern and eastern Asia, living
    standards in, 6, 12, 28, 29, 33, 37,
    38, 40, 42, 44
southern and eastern Asia, settlement
    patterns of, 6, 11, 12, 16, 19, 22,
    26, 28, 33, 37, 40
southern and eastern Asia, unrest in,
    18, 30, 31, 41, 44, 45
southern and eastern Asia, weather
    patterns of, 8, 10, 11, 15, 16, 19,
    23, 26, 32, 36-37, 38, 40
South Korea, 18-19, 20
Soviet Union, former, 17, 18
Sri Lanka, 41

T

Taiwan, 6, 15
Thailand, 31, 32-33
Tibet, 6, 10, 43
tourism, 14, 24, 41

U

United States, 18, 28

V

Vietnam, 30-31, 33
volcanic eruptions, 22, 24

W

World War II, 18, 30